S0-ARN-876

MICROSOFT WINDOWS 95

Introductory Concepts and Techniques

Gary B. Shelly
Thomas J. Cashman
Steven G. Forsythe

Contributing Author
Tim J. Walker

SHELLY
CASHMAN
SERIES®

boyd & fraser

boyd & fraser

A DIVISION OF COURSE TECHNOLOGY
ONE MAIN STREET
CAMBRIDGE MA 02142

An International Thomson Publishing Company I(T)P

Albany • Bonn • Boston • Cincinnati • London • Madrid • Melbourne
Mexico City • New York • Paris • San Francisco • Tokyo • Toronto • Washington

© 1996 boyd & fraser publishing company
A Division of Course Technology
One Corporate Place • 55 Ferncroft Road
Danvers, Massachusetts 01923-4016

COURSE
TECHNOLOGY

 International Thomson Publishing
boyd & fraser publishing company is an ITP company.
The ITP trademark is used under license.

Printed in the United States of America

For more information, contact boyd & fraser publishing company:

boyd & fraser publishing company
A Division of Course Technology
One Corporate Place • 55 Ferncroft Road
Danvers, Massachusetts 01923-4016, USA

International Thomson Publishing Europe
Berkshire House
168-173 High Holborn
London, WC1V 7AA, United Kingdom

Thomas Nelson Australia
102 Dodds Street
South Melbourne
Victoria 3205 Australia

Nelson Canada
1120 Birchmont Road
Scarborough, Ontario
Canada M1K 5G4

International Thomson Editores
Campos Eliseos 385, Piso 7
Colonia Polanco
11560 Mexico D.F. Mexico

International Thomson Publishing GmbH
Konigswinterer Strasse 418
53227 Bonn, Germany

International Thomson Publishing Asia
Block 211, Henderson Road #08-03
Henderson Industrial Park
Singapore 0315

International Thomson Publishing Japan
Hirakawa-cho Kyowa Building, 3F
2-2-1 Hirakawa-cho, Chiyoda-ku
Tokyo 102, Japan

All rights reserved. No part of this work may be reproduced or used in any form or by any means—
graphic, electronic, or mechanical, including photocopying, recording, taping, or information and retrieval systems—
without prior written permission from the publisher.

ISBN 0-7895-1283-1

SHELLY CASHMAN SERIES® and **Custom Edition**® are trademarks of International Thomson Publishing, Inc. Names of all other products mentioned herein are used for identification purposes only and may be trademarks and/or registered trademarks of their respective owners. International Thomson Publishing, Inc. and boyd & fraser publishing company disclaim any affiliation, association, or connection with, or sponsorship or endorsement by such owners.

Photo Credits: *Project 1 page 1.4* Bill Gates, © Matthew McVay, Stock Boston; Seattle Skyline, © Paul Conklin, PhotoEdit; *page 1.5* International Business Machines Corp.; *Project 2 page 2.3* Quantum Corp.

7 8 9 10   BC   09

MICROSOFT WINDOWS 95

Introductory Concepts and Techniques

CONTENTS

Preface

Shelly Cashman Series® Microsoft Windows 95 Books

The Shelly Cashman Series® Microsoft Windows 95 books reinforce the fact that you make the right choice when you use a Shelly Cashman Series book. The Shelly Cashman Series Microsoft Windows 3.1 books were used by more schools and more students than any other series in textbook publishing. Yet the Shelly Cashman Series team wanted to produce even better books for Windows 95, so the books were thoroughly redesigned to present material in an even easier-to-understand format. Features such as Other Ways and More Abouts were added to give in-depth knowledge to the student. The opening of each project provides a fascinating perspective of the subject covered in the project. Completely redesigned student assignments include the unique Cases and Places. This book provides the finest educational experience ever for a student learning about computer software.

Objectives of This Textbook

Microsoft Windows 95: Introductory Concepts and Techniques is intended for a course that includes an introduction to Windows 95. No computer experience is assumed. The objectives of this book are:

▶ To provide an overview of Windows 95 that students can build on

▶ To expose students to real-world examples and procedures that will prepare them to use Windows 95

When students complete the course using this textbook, they will have a firm knowledge and understanding of Windows 95.

The Shelly Cashman Approach

Features of the Shelly Cashman Series Windows 95 books include:

▶ Project Orientation: Each project in the book presents ways to use Windows 95 through the unique Shelly Cashman Series screen-by-screen, step-by-step approach.

▶ Screen-by-Screen, Step-by-Step Instructions: Each of the tasks required to complete a project is identified throughout the development of the project. Then, steps to accomplish the task are specified. The steps are accompanied by screens. The student is not told to perform a step without seeing the result of the step on a color screen. Hence, students learn from this book the same as if they were using a computer.

▶ Thoroughly Tested Projects: The computer screens in the Shelly Cashman Series Windows 95 books are shot directly from the author's computer. The screen is shot immediately after the author performs the step specified in the text. Therefore, every screen in the book is correct because it is produced only after performing a specific step, resulting in unprecedented quality in a computer textbook.

▶ **Multiple Ways to Use the Book:** The book can be used in a variety of ways, including: (a) Lecture and textbook approach – The instructor lectures on the material in the book. The student reads and studies the material and then applies the knowledge to an application on the computer; (b) Tutorial approach – The student performs each specified step on a computer. At the end of the project, the student has solved the problem and is ready to solve comparable student assignments; (c) Other approaches – Many teachers lecture on the material and then require their students to perform each step in the project, reinforcing the material lectured. The students then complete one or more of the In the Lab exercises; and (d) Reference – Each task in a project is clearly identified. Therefore, the material serves as a complete reference.

▶ **Windows/Graphical User Interface Approach:** Windows 95 provides a graphical user interface and all the examples in this book use this interface. Thus, the mouse is the preferred user communication tool. The secondary, or right, mouse button is used extensively.

▶ **Other Ways Boxes for Reference:** Windows 95 provides a wide variety of ways to carry out a given task. The Other Ways boxes displayed at the end of most of the step-by-step sequences specify the other ways to do the task completed in the steps. Thus, the steps and the Other Ways box make a comprehensive reference unit. You no longer have to reference tables at the end of a chapter or the end of a book.

Organization of This Textbook

Microsoft Windows 95: Introductory Concepts and Techniques consists of two projects, as follows:

Project 1 - Fundamentals of Using Windows 95   In Project 1, the student learns about user interfaces and Microsoft Windows 95. Topics include: using the Windows 95 desktop as a work area; mouse operations; maximizing and minimizing windows; sizing and scrolling windows; creating a document by starting an application program; saving a document on disk; printing a document; closing a program; modifying a document; using Windows Help; and shutting down Windows 95.

Project 2 - Using Windows Explorer   In Project 2, students are introduced to Windows Explorer. Topics include displaying the contents of a folder; expanding and collapsing a folder; changing the view; selecting and copying a group of files; creating, renaming, and deleting a folder; and renaming and deleting a file.

End-of-Project Student Activities

A notable strength of the Shelly Cashman Series Windows 95 books is the extensive student activities at the end of each project. Well-structured student activities can make the difference between students merely participating in a class and students retaining the information they learn. These activities include all of the following sections.

▶ **What You Should Know** A listing of the tasks completed within a project together with the pages where the step-by-step, screen-by-screen explanations appear. This section provides a perfect study review for the student.

▶ **Test Your Knowledge** These activities are designed to determine the student's understanding of the material in the project. Included are true/false questions, multiple-choice questions, and one or more other unique activities.

▶ **Use Help** Any user of Windows 95 must know how to use Help. Therefore, this book contains exercises that require students to use Help. These exercises alone distinguish the Shelly Cashman Series from any other set of Windows 95 instructional materials.

▶ **In the Lab** These assignments require the student to apply the knowledge gained in the project to solve problems on a computer.

▶ **Cases and Places** Unique case studies allow students to apply their knowledge to real-world situations. In addition, these case studies provide subjects for research papers based on information gained from a resource such as the Internet.

Instructor's Support Package

A comprehensive instructor's support package accompanies this textbook in the form of an Instructor's Manual and CD-ROM. Most of the support materials on the CD-ROM also are available through the Teaching Resources link on the Shelly Cashman Online home page (http://www.bf.com/scseries.html).

▶ **Instructor's Manual** The Instructor's Manual contains the following:

- Detailed lesson plans

- Answers to all the student exercises at the end of the projects

- A test bank of true/false, multiple-choice, and fill-in-the-blank questions

▶ **CD-ROM** The CD-ROM includes the following:

- **Figures on CD-ROM** Illustrations for every screen in the textbook.

- **ElecMan** ElecMan stands for *Elec*tronic *Man*ual. ElecMan is a digital Instructor's Manual. The files allow you to modify the lecture notes or generate quizzes and exams from the test bank using your word processor.

- **Course Test Manager** Designed by Course Technology, this cutting edge Windows-based testing software helps instructors design and administer tests and pre-tests. The full-featured online program permits students to take tests at the computer where their grades are computed immediately following completion of the exam. Automatic statistics collection, student guides customized to the student's performance, and printed tests are only a few of the features.

Shelly Cashman Online

Shelly Cashman Online is a World Wide Web service available to instructors and students of computer education. Visit Shelly Cashman Online at http://www.bf.com/scseries.html. Shelly Cashman Online is divided into four areas:

▶ **Series Information** Information on the Shelly Cashman Series products.

▶ **The Community** Opportunities to discuss your course and your ideas with instructors in your field and with the Shelly Cashman Series team.

▶ **Teaching Resources** This area includes password-protected data from Instructor's Floppy Disks that can be downloaded, course outlines, teaching tips, and materials such as ElecMan.

▶ **Student Center** Dedicated to students learning about computers with Shelly Cashman Series textbooks and software. This area includes cool links, data from Student's Floppy Disks that can be downloaded, and much more.

Acknowledgments

The Shelly Cashman Series would not be the leading computer education series without the contributions of outstanding publishing professionals. First, and foremost, among them is Becky Herrington, director of production and designer. She is the heart and soul of the Shelly Cashman Series, and it is only through her leadership, dedication, and tireless efforts that superior products are made possible. Becky created and produced the award-winning Windows 95 series of books.

Under Becky's direction, the following individuals made significant contributions to these books: Peter Schiller, production manager; Ginny Harvey, series administrator and manuscript editor; Ken Russo, senior illustrator and cover artist; Mike Bodnar, Stephanie Nance, Greg Herrington, and Dave Bonnewitz, Quark artists and illustrators; Patti Garbarino, editorial assistant; Jeanne Black, Quark expert; Cristina Haley, indexer; Sarah Evertson of Image Quest, photo researcher; Henry Blackham, cover photographer; and Kent Lauer, cover glass work. Special mention must go to Suzanne Biron, Becky Herrington, and Michael Gregson for the outstanding book design, and to Becky Herrington for the cover design.

Special recognition also must go to Tracy Murphy, series associate editor and Mike Campbell, World Wide Web and multimedia guru. The efforts of Jim Quasney, series editor, are unmatched in publishing. Without Jim, none of this happens. Particular thanks go to Tom Walker, president of boyd & fraser publishing company. His creativity, support, and understanding are vital ingredients to the success of the Shelly Cashman Series.

Gary B. Shelly
Thomas J. Cashman
Steven G. Forsythe

▶ PROJECT ONE

FUNDAMENTALS OF USING WINDOWS 95

Objectives:

You will have mastered the material in this project when you can:

▶ Describe Microsoft Windows 95
▶ Describe a user interface
▶ Identify the objects on the Microsoft Windows 95 desktop
▶ Perform the basic mouse operations: point, click, right-click, double-click, drag, and right-drag
▶ Open a Windows 95 window
▶ Maximize, minimize, and restore a Windows 95 window
▶ Close a Windows 95 window
▶ Resize a window
▶ Scroll in a window
▶ Move a window on the Windows 95 desktop
▶ Understand keyboard shortcut notation
▶ Start an application program
▶ Create a written document
▶ Save a document on disk
▶ Print a document
▶ Close an application program
▶ Modify a document stored on disk
▶ Use Windows 95 Help
▶ Shut down Windows 95

▶ PROJECT TWO

USING WINDOWS EXPLORER

Objectives:

You will have mastered the material in this project when you can:

▶ Start Windows Explorer
▶ Understand the elements of the Exploring – My Computer window
▶ Display the contents of a folder
▶ Expand and collapse a folder
▶ Change the view
▶ Select and copy one file or a group of files
▶ Create, rename, and delete a folder
▶ Rename and delete a file

Project 1

A $14 Billion Mistake?

Digital Research officials would not yield to IBM's demands

H ave you ever missed a meeting you should have attended but something else was more important? Did you lose $14 billion dollars because you were absent? Gary Kildall might have.

In the 1970s, Kildall's company, Digital Research, had developed an operating system called CP/M that was used on most microcomputers except the Apple II. Kildall was a leader in the microcomputer software business. Then, in 1980, IBM came calling.

Having decided to build a personal computer, IBM approached Bill Gates, president of a small company called Microsoft, in Redmond, Washington, to create the operating system. Gates demurred, suggesting IBM contact Kildall.

Bill Gates

MICROSOFT

MS-DOS

SEATTLE COMPUTER PRODUCTS

When IBM arrived for the meeting in Pacific Grove, California, Kildall was off flying his airplane. The reasons are not entirely clear. Some say Kildall was a free spirit and not inclined to do business with the monolithic IBM. Kildall claimed he was flying to another important meeting.

Without Kildall at the meeting, IBM insisted on knowing everything about CP/M while disclosing nothing about its new computer. Fearing IBM would steal their secrets, Digital Research officials would not yield to IBM's demands. Rebuffed, IBM scurried back to Gates.

Sensing an opportunity, Gates agreed to provide an operating system to IBM even though he had no idea how. It just so happened, however, that a small company named Seattle Computer Products, almost next door to Microsoft, was writing an operating system called QDOS v0.110 (QDOS stood for Quick and Dirty Operating System).

Gates learned of QDOS and approached Seattle Computer Products to ask if the operating system was for sale. For a few favors and a little money, Microsoft, in December 1980, acquired non-exclusive rights to QDOS. Later, Microsoft acquired all rights and renamed the operating system MS-DOS. Seattle Computer Products received about $1 million.

Microsoft made substantial changes to MS-DOS and when IBM announced its personal computer in August 1981, MS-DOS was the operating system. The IBM machine was an instant hit. Microsoft sold millions of copies of MS-DOS and grew to be the largest software company in the world. Bill Gates became the world's richest man, with assets in excess of $14 billion dollars.

And Gary Kildall? He continued to develop software at Digital Research. Eventually, Digital Research was sold to Novell, Inc. In the summer of 1994, Kildall died. He left a legacy as an early pioneer who made a significant contribution to microcomputing, but perhaps his most memorable act was missing a meeting.

QDOS

```
Enter today's date (m-d-y): 8-4-1981

The IBM Personal Computer DOS
Version 1.00 (C)Copyright IBM Corp 1981

A>
```

Courtesy of Tim Paterson,
reprinted by permission of Microsoft Corporation.

The Microsoft Disk Operating System, or MS-DOS, was shipped as PC-DOS on the original IBM Personal Computer and later with many IBM compatible machines. Like other operating systems, MS-DOS oversees all the functions of a computer. Various upgrades to MS-DOS and further product refinements led to the release of Windows, an operating system that uses a graphical user interface. Microsoft's current version of Windows, released in August of 1995, is called Windows 95.

©Copyright 1995 The Road Ahead, William H. Gates III. All rights reserved.

CP/M

GARY KILDALL

IBM

DIGITAL RESEARCH

Microsoft sold millions of copies of MS-DOS and grew to be the largest software company in the world

Project 1

Microsoft *Windows 95*

Fundamentals of Using Windows 95

Case Perspective

Need: Each day millions of Windows 95 users turn on their computers, whether at home, in the office, at school, on an airplane, or at the beach. When the computer starts, the first image on the monitor is the Windows 95 desktop. If these users did not know how to start application programs from the desktop, manipulate files and images on the desktop, and preserve the work accomplished, their computers would be useless. You have just acquired a computer containing Windows 95. Your task is to learn the basics of Windows 95 so your computer will be useful to you.

Introduction

An **operating system** is the set of computer instructions, called a computer program, that controls the allocation of computer hardware such as memory, disk devices, printers, and CD-ROM drives, and provides the capability for you to communicate with your computer. The most popular and widely used operating system for personal computers is **Microsoft Windows. Microsoft Windows 95** (called Windows 95 for the rest of this book), the newest version of Microsoft Windows, allows you to easily communicate with and control your computer. Windows 95 is easier to use and more efficient than previous versions of Windows and can be customized to fit individual needs. Windows 95 simplifies the process of working with documents and applications, transferring data between documents, and organizing the manner in which you interact with your computer.

In Project 1, you will learn about Windows 95 and how to use the Windows 95 user interface.

Microsoft Windows 95

Microsoft Windows 95 is an operating system that performs every function necessary for you to communicate with and use your computer. Unlike previous versions of Windows, no associated operating system is required. Windows 95 is called a **32-bit operating system** because it uses 32 bits for addressing and other purposes, which means the operating system can address more than four gigabytes of RAM and perform tasks faster than older operating systems.

Windows 95 is designed to be compatible with all existing **application programs**, which are programs that perform an application-related function such as word processing. To use the application programs that can be executed under Windows 95, you must know about the Windows 95 user interface.

What Is a User Interface?

A **user interface** is the combination of hardware and software that you use to communicate with and control your computer. Through the user interface, you are able to make selections on your computer, request information from your computer, and respond to messages displayed by your computer. Thus, a user interface provides the means for dialogue between you and your computer.

Hardware and software together form the user interface. Among the hardware devices associated with a user interface are the monitor, keyboard, and mouse (Figure 1-1). The monitor displays messages and provides information. You respond by entering data in the form of a command or other response using the keyboard or mouse. Among the responses available to you are responses that specify what application program to run, what document to open, when to print, and where to store data for future use.

The computer software associated with the user interface consists of the programs that engage you in dialogue (Figure 1-1). The computer software determines the messages you receive, the manner in which you should respond, and the actions that occur based on your responses.

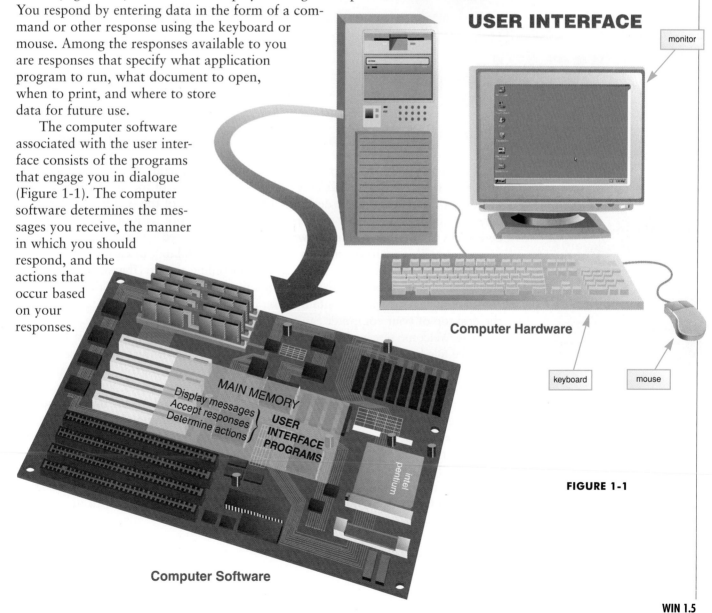

USER INTERFACE

monitor

Computer Hardware

keyboard   mouse

MAIN MEMORY
Display messages
Accept responses   USER
Determine actions   INTERFACE
PROGRAMS

intel pentium

Computer Software

FIGURE 1-1

The goal of an effective user interface is to be **user friendly**, meaning that the software can be used easily by individuals with limited training. Research studies have indicated that the use of graphics can play an important role in aiding users to interact effectively with a computer. A **graphical user interface**, or **GUI** (pronounced gooey), is a user interface that displays graphics in addition to text when it communicates with the user.

The Windows 95 graphical user interface was carefully designed to be easier to set up, simpler to learn, and faster and more powerful than previous versions of Microsoft Windows.

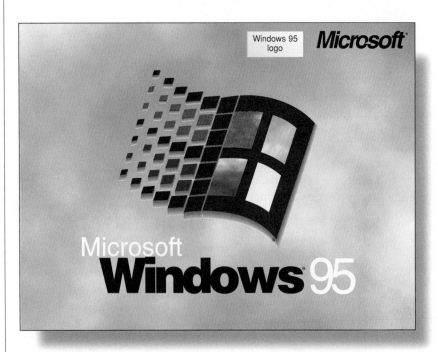

FIGURE 1-2

Starting Microsoft Windows 95

When you turn on your computer, an introductory screen consisting of the Windows 95 logo and the Microsoft Windows 95 name displays on a blue sky and clouds background (Figure 1-2).

The screen clears and several items display on a background called the **desktop**. The default color of the desktop background is green, but your computer may display a different color. Your screen might display as shown in Figure 1-3. It also might display without the Welcome screen shown in Figure 1-3.

The items on the desktop in Figure 1-3 include six icons and their names on the left of the desktop, the Welcome screen in the center of the desktop, and the taskbar at the bottom of the desktop. Through the use of the six **icons**, you can view the contents of your computer (**My Computer**), work with other computers connected to your computer (**Network Neighborhood**), receive and send electronic faxes and mail (e-mail) from or to other computers (**Inbox**), discard unneeded objects (**Recycle Bin**), connect to the Microsoft online service (**The Microsoft Network**), and transfer data to and from a portable computer (**My Briefcase**). Your computer's desktop might contain more, fewer, or some different icons because the desktop of your computer can be customized.

The Welcome screen that might display on your desktop is shown in Figure 1-3. The **title bar**, which is dark blue in color at the top of the screen, identifies the name of the screen (Welcome) and contains the Close button, which can be used to close the Welcome screen. In the Welcome screen, a welcome message (Welcome to Windows 95) displays together with a helpful tip for using Windows 95, a check box containing a check mark, and several command buttons. The **check box** represents an option to display the Welcome screen each time Windows 95 starts that you can turn on or turn off. The **command buttons** allow you to perform different operations such as displaying the next tip or closing the screen.

Below the screen is the mouse pointer. On the desktop, the **mouse pointer** is the shape of a block arrow. The mouse pointer allows you to point to items on the desktop.

◆**More** *About*
the Windows 95 Interface

Thousands of hours were spent developing the Windows 95 graphical user interface. Of tremendous importance in the development were Microsoft's usability labs, where everyone from raw beginners to experts interacted with many different versions of the interface. The taskbar and other significant features of the interface emerged from the experiences in these labs.

The **taskbar** at the bottom of the screen in Figure 1-3 contains the Start button, the Welcome button, and the Tray status area. The **Start button** provides an entry point to begin using the features of Windows 95, the Welcome button indicates the Welcome screen is open on the desktop, and the current time (6:06 PM) displays in the Tray status area.

Nearly every item on the Windows 95 desktop is considered an object. Even the desktop itself is an object. Every **object** has properties. The **properties** of an object are unique to that specific object and may affect what can be done to the object or what the object does. For example, the properties of an object may be the color of the object, such as the color of the desktop.

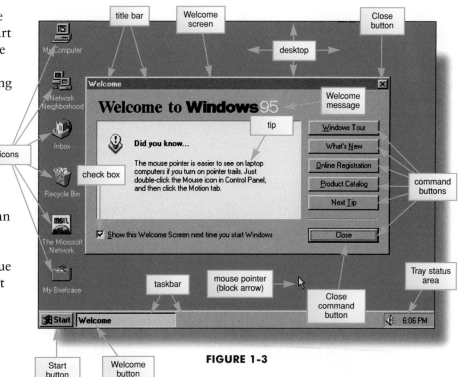

FIGURE 1-3

Closing the Welcome Screen

As noted, the Welcome screen might display when you start Windows 95. If the Welcome screen does display on the desktop, normally you should close it prior to beginning any other operations using Windows 95. To close the Welcome screen, complete the following step.

TO CLOSE THE WELCOME SCREEN

Step 1: Press the ESC key on the keyboard as shown in Figure 1-4.

The Welcome screen closes.

The Desktop as a Work Area

The Windows 95 desktop and the objects on the desktop were designed to emulate a work area in an office or at home. The Windows desktop may be thought of as an electronic version of the top of your desk. You can move objects around on the desktop, look at them and then put them aside, and so on. In Project 1, you will learn how to interact with and communicate with the Windows 95 desktop.

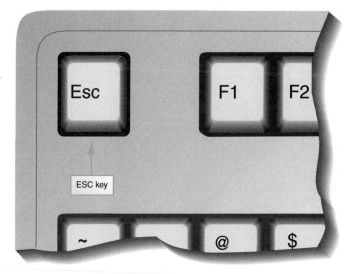

FIGURE 1-4

More *About* **the Mouse**

The mouse, though invented in the 1960's, was not widely used until the Apple Macintosh computer became available in 1984. Even then, some high-brows called mouse users "wimps." Today, the mouse is an indispensable tool for every computer user.

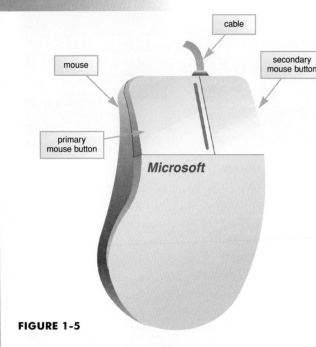

cable

mouse

secondary mouse button

primary mouse button

Microsoft

FIGURE 1-5

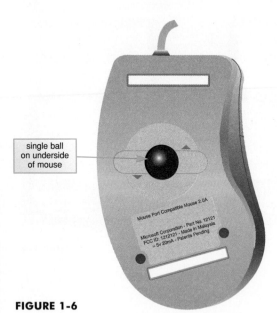

single ball on underside of mouse

FIGURE 1-6

Communicating with Microsoft Windows 95

The Windows 95 interface provides the means for dialogue between you and your computer. Part of this dialogue involves your requesting information from your computer and responding to messages displayed by your computer. You can request information and respond to messages using either a mouse or a keyboard.

Mouse Operations

A **mouse** is a pointing device used with Windows 95 that is attached to the computer by a cable. It contains two buttons — the primary mouse button and the secondary mouse button (Figure 1-5). The **primary mouse button** is typically the left mouse button and the **secondary mouse button** is typically the right mouse button although Windows 95 allows you to switch them. In this book, the left mouse button is the primary mouse button and the right mouse button is the secondary mouse button.

Using the mouse, you can perform the following operations: (1) point; (2) click; (3) right-click; (4) double-click; (5) drag; and (6) right-drag. These operations are demonstrated on the following pages.

Point and Click

Point means you move the mouse across a flat surface until the mouse pointer rests on the item of choice on the desktop. As you move the mouse across a flat surface, the movement of a ball on the underside of the mouse (Figure 1-6) is electronically sensed, and the mouse pointer moves across the desktop in the same direction.

Click means you press and release the primary mouse button, which in this book is the left mouse button. In most cases, you must point to an item before you click. To become acquainted with the use of a mouse, perform the following steps to point to and click various objects on the desktop.

Steps **To Point and Click**

1 **Point to the Start button on the taskbar by moving the mouse across a flat surface until the mouse pointer rests on the Start button.**

*The mouse pointer points to the Start button and a **ToolTip** (Click here to begin) displays (Figure 1-7). The ToolTip, which provides instructions, displays on the desktop for approximately five seconds.*

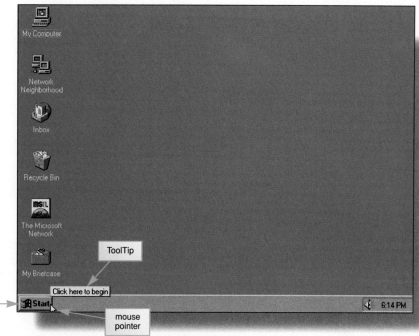

FIGURE 1-7

2 **Click the Start button on the taskbar by pressing and releasing the left mouse button.**

*Windows 95 opens the **Start menu** and indents the Start button (Figure 1-8). A **menu** is a list of related commands. Nine commands display on the Start menu. A **command** directs Windows 95 to perform a specific action such as opening another menu or shutting down the operating system. Each command consists of an icon and a command name. Some commands (Run and Shut Down) are followed by an **ellipsis** (...) to indicate Windows 95 requires more information before executing the command. Other commands (Programs, Documents, Settings, and Find) are followed by a **right arrow**. A right arrow indicates that pointing to the command will open a submenu containing more commands.*

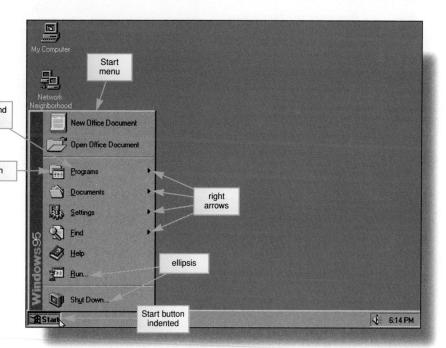

FIGURE 1-8

3 **Point to Programs on the Start menu.**

When you point to Programs, Windows 95 highlights the Programs command on the Start menu and opens the **Programs** **submenu** (Figure 1-9). A **submenu** is a menu that displays when you point to a command that is followed by a right arrow.

FIGURE 1-9

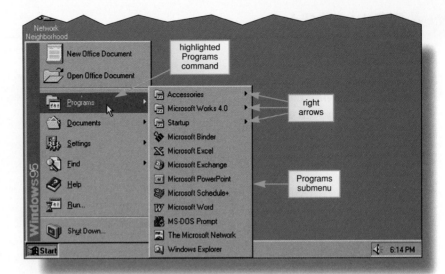

4 **Point to an open area of the desktop and then click the open area of the desktop.**

Windows 95 closes the Start menu and the Programs submenu (Figure 1-10). The mouse pointer points to the desktop. To close a menu anytime, click anywhere on the desktop except the menu itself. The Start button is not indented.

FIGURE 1-10

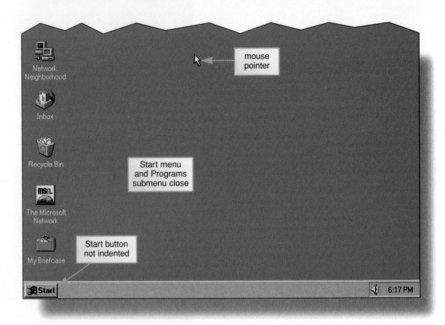

More *About* **Buttons**

Buttons on the desktop and in programs are in integral part of Windows 95. When you point to them, their function displays in a ToolTip. When you click them, they appear to indent on the screen to mimic what would happen if you pushed an actual button. All buttons in Windows 95 behave in the same manner.

Notice in Figure 1-9 that whenever you point to a command on a menu, the command is highlighted.

When you click an object such as the Start button in Figure 1-8 on the previous page, you must point to the object before you click. In the steps that follow, the instruction that directs you to point to a particular item and then click is, Click the particular item. For example, Click the Start button, means point to the Start button and then click.

Right-Click

Right-click means you press and release the secondary mouse button, which in this book is the right mouse button. As when you use the primary mouse button, normally you will point to an object on the screen prior to right-clicking. Perform the following steps to right-click the desktop.

Steps To Right-Click

1 **Point to an open area on the desktop and press and release the right mouse button.**

*Windows 95 displays a context-sensitive menu containing six commands (Figure 1-11). Right-clicking an object, such as the desktop, opens a **context-sensitive menu** (also referred to as a **shortcut menu** or an **object menu**) that contains a set of commands specifically for use with that object. The Paste command in Figure 1-11 is dimmed, meaning that command cannot be used at the current time.*

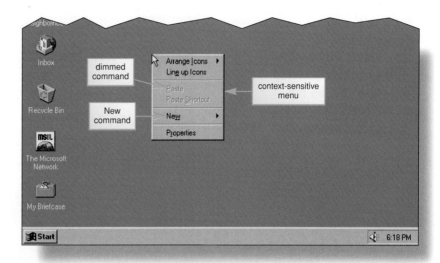

FIGURE 1-11

2 **Point to New on the context-sensitive menu.**

*When you move the mouse pointer to the New command, Windows 95 highlights the New command and opens the **New submenu** (Figure 1-12). The New submenu contains a variety of commands. The number of commands and the actual commands that display on your computer might be different.*

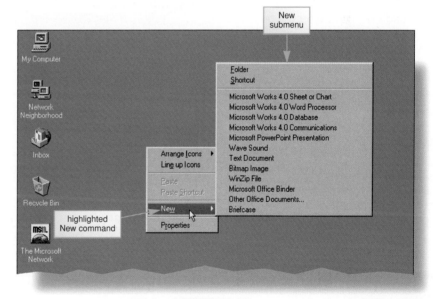

3 **Point to an open area of the desktop and click the open area to remove the context-sensitive menu and the New submenu.**

FIGURE 1-12

Whenever you right-click an object, a context-sensitive, or shortcut, menu will display. As you will see, the use of shortcut menus speeds up your work and adds flexibility to your interface with the computer.

Double-Click

Double-click means you quickly press and release the left mouse button twice without moving the mouse. In most cases, you must point to an item before you double-click. Perform the step on the next page to open the My Computer window on the desktop by double-clicking the My Computer icon.

Steps To Open a Window by Double-Clicking

1 **Point to the My Computer icon on the desktop and double-click by quickly pressing and releasing the left mouse button twice without moving the mouse.**

*Windows 95 opens the My Computer window and adds the My Computer button to the taskbar (Figure 1-13). The My Computer window is the active window. The **active window** is the window currently being used. Whenever you double-click an object that can be opened, Windows 95 will open the object; and the open object will be identified by a button on the taskbar. The active window is identified by the indented button.*

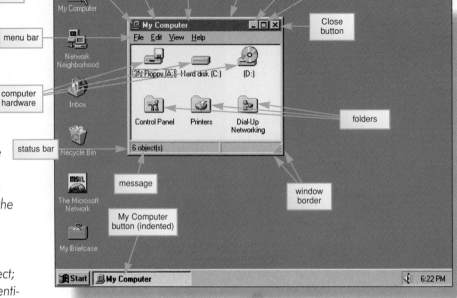

FIGURE 1-13

More *About* **Double-Clicking**

Double-clicking is the most difficult mouse skill to learn. Many people have a tendency to move the mouse before they click a second time, even when they do not want to move the mouse. You should find, however, that with a little practice double-clicking becomes quite natural.

More *About* **My Computer**

The trade press and media have poked fun at the icon name, My Computer. One wag said no one should use Windows 95 for more than five minutes without changing the name (which is easily done). Microsoft responds that in its usability labs, My Computer was the most easily understood name by beginning computer users.

My Computer Window

The thin line, or **window border**, surrounding the My Computer window in Figure 1-13 determines its shape and size. The **title bar** at the top of the window contains a small icon that is the same as the icon on the desktop and the **window title** (My Computer) that identifies the window. The color of the title bar (dark blue) and the indented My Computer button on the taskbar indicate the My Computer window is the active window. The color of the active window on your computer might be different from the dark blue color.

Clicking the icon at the left on the title bar will open the Control menu, which contains commands to carry out actions associated with the My Computer window. At the right on the title bar are three buttons, the Minimize button, the Maximize button, and the Close button, that can be used to specify the size of the window and can close the window.

The **menu bar**, a horizontal bar below the title bar of a window (see Figure 1-13), contains a list of menu names for the My Computer window: File, Edit, View, and Help. One letter in each menu name is underlined. You can open a menu by clicking the menu name on the menu bar.

Six icons display in the My Computer window. A name below each icon identifies the icon. The three icons in the top row represent a 3½ floppy disk drive (3½ Floppy [A:]), a hard disk drive (Hard disk [C:]), and a CD-ROM drive ([D:]). The contents of the My Computer window on your computer might be different than shown in Figure 1-13.

The icons in the second row are folders. A **folder** is an object created to contain related documents, applications, and other folders. A folder in Windows 95 contains items in much the same way a folder on your desk contains items. If you double-click a folder, the items within the folder display in a window. A message at the left of the **status bar** located at the bottom of the window indicates the window contains six objects (see Figure 1-13).

Minimize Button

Two buttons on the title bar of a window, the Minimize button and the Maximize button, allow you to control the way a window displays or does not display on the desktop. When you click the **Minimize button** (see Figure 1-13), the My Computer window no longer displays on the desktop and the indented My Computer button on the taskbar changes to a non-indented button. A minimized window or application program is still open but it does not display on the screen. To minimize and then redisplay the My Computer window, complete the following steps.

 Steps To Minimize and Redisplay a Window

More *About*
Minimizing
Windows

Window management on the Windows 95 desktop is important in order to keep the desktop uncluttered. You will find yourself frequently minimizing windows, and then later reopening them with a click of a button on the taskbar.

1 **Point to the Minimize button on the title bar of the My Computer window.**

The mouse pointer points to the Minimize button on the My Computer window title bar (Figure 1-14). The My Computer button on the taskbar is indented.

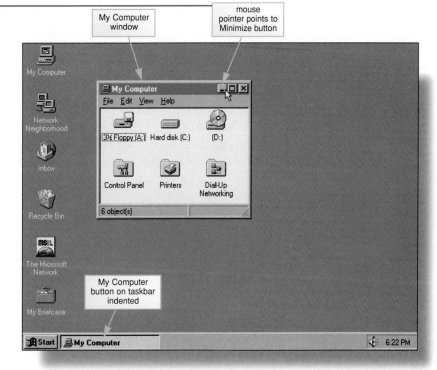

FIGURE 1-14

2 **Click the Minimize button.**

The My Computer window disappears from the desktop and the My Computer button on the taskbar changes to a non-indented button (Figure 1-15).

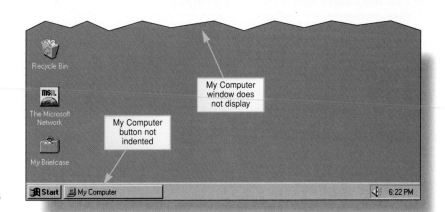

FIGURE 1-15

3 **Click the My Computer button on the taskbar.**

The My Computer window displays on the desktop in the same place and size as before it was minimized (Figure 1-16). In addition, the My Computer window is the active window because it contains the dark blue title bar and the My Computer button on the taskbar is indented.

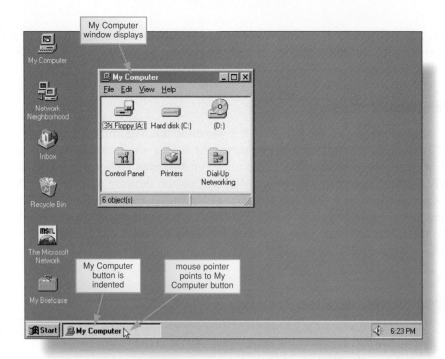

FIGURE 1-16

Whenever a window is minimized, it does not display on the desktop but a non-indented button for the window does display on the taskbar. Whenever you want a window that has been minimized to display and be the active window, click the window's button on the taskbar.

Maximize and Restore Buttons

The **Maximize button** maximizes a window so the window fills the entire screen, making it easier to see the contents of the window. When a window is maximized, the **Restore button** replaces the Maximize button on the title bar. Clicking the Restore button will return the window to its size before maximizing. To maximize and restore the My Computer window, complete the following steps.

More *About*
Maximizing Windows

Many application programs run in a maximized window by default. Often you will find that you want to work with maximized windows.

Steps **To Maximize and Restore a Window**

1 **Point to the Maximize button on the title bar of the My Computer window.**

The mouse pointer points to the Maximize button on the title bar of the My Computer window (Figure 1-17).

FIGURE 1-17

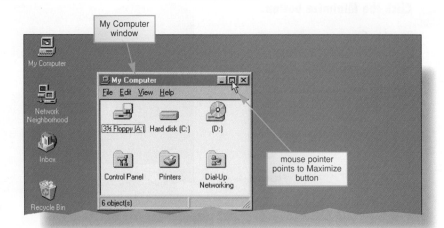

2 **Click the Maximize button.**

The My Computer window expands so it and the taskbar fill the entire screen (Figure 1-18). The Restore button replaces the Maximize button. The My Computer button on the taskbar does not change. The My Computer window is still the active window.

FIGURE 1-18

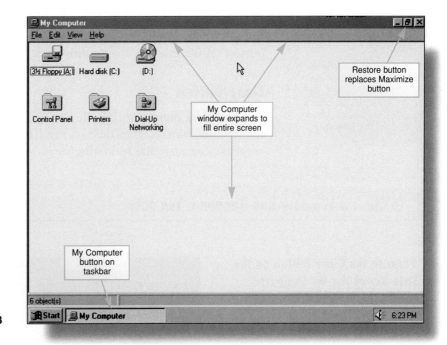

3 **Point to the Restore button on the title bar of the My Computer window.**

The mouse pointer points to the Restore button on the title bar of the My Computer window (Figure 1-19).

FIGURE 1-19

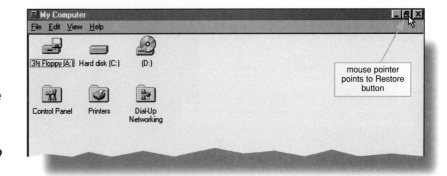

4 **Click the Restore button.**

The My Computer window returns to the size and position it occupied before being maximized (Figure 1-20). The My Computer button on the taskbar does not change. The Maximize button replaces the Restore button.

FIGURE 1-20

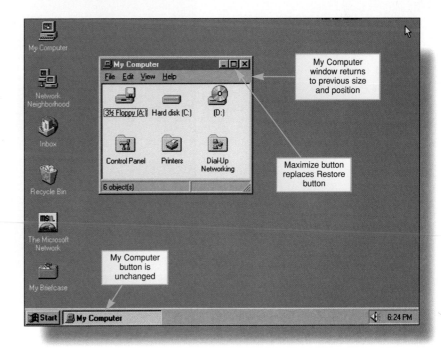

More *About*
the Close Button

The Close button is a new inno-
vation for Windows 95. In previous versions of Windows, the
user had to either double-click a
button or click a command from
a menu to close the window.

When a window is maximized, you can also minimize the window by clicking the Minimize button. If, after minimizing the window, you click the window button on the taskbar, the window will return to its maximized size.

Close Button

The **Close button** on the title bar of a window closes the window and removes the window button from the taskbar. To close and then reopen the My Computer window, complete the following steps.

Steps **To Close a Window and Reopen a Window**

1 **Point to the Close button on the title bar of the My Computer window.**

The mouse pointer points to the Close button on the title bar of the My Computer window (Figure 1-21).

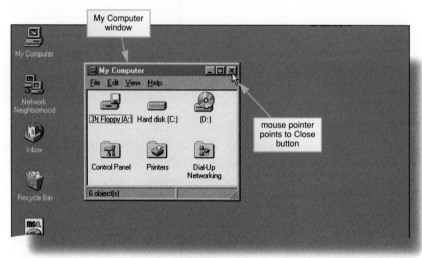

FIGURE 1-21

2 **Click the Close button.**

The My Computer window closes and the My Computer button no longer displays on the taskbar (Figure 1-22).

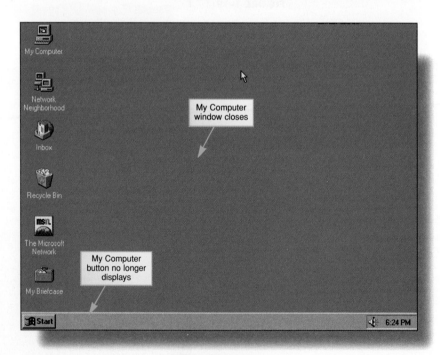

FIGURE 1-22

3 **Point to and double-click the My Computer icon on the desktop.**

The My Computer window opens and displays on the screen (Figure 1-23). The My Computer button displays on the taskbar.

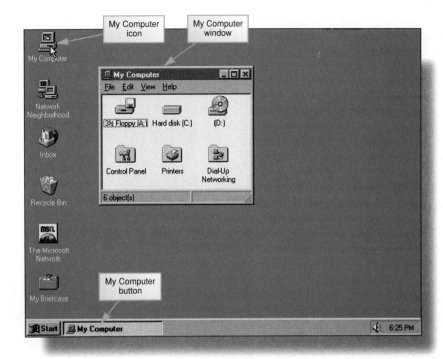

FIGURE 1-23

Drag

Drag means you point to an item, hold down the left mouse button, move the item to the desired location on the screen, and then release the left mouse button. You can move any open window to another location on the desktop by pointing to the title bar of the window and dragging the window. To drag the My Computer window, perform the following steps.

 Steps **To Move an Object by Dragging**

1 **Point to the My Computer window title bar.**

The mouse pointer points to the My Computer window title bar (Figure 1-24).

> **M**ore *About*
> **Dragging**
>
> Dragging is the second-most difficult skill to learn with a mouse. You may want to practice dragging a few times so you are comfortable with it.

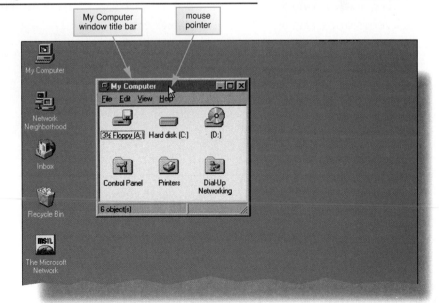

FIGURE 1-24

2 **Hold down the left mouse button and then move the mouse so the window outline moves to the center of the desktop (do not release the left mouse button).**

As you drag the My Computer window, Windows 95 displays an outline of the window (Figure 1-25). The outline, which can be positioned anywhere on the desktop, specifies where the window will display when you release the left mouse button.

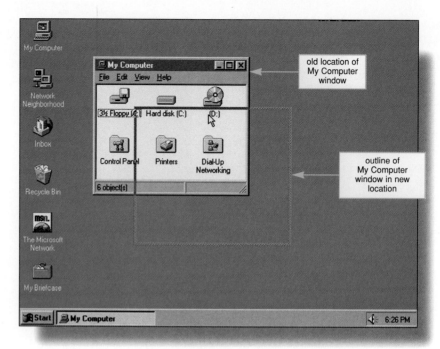

FIGURE 1-25

3 **Release the left mouse button.**

Windows 95 moves the My Computer window to the location the outline occupied prior to releasing the left mouse button (Figure 1-26).

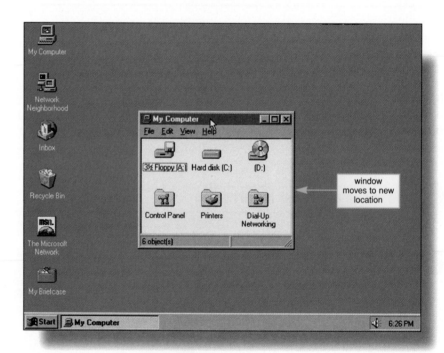

FIGURE 1-26

Sizing a Window by Dragging

You can use dragging for more than just moving an item or object. For example, you can drag the border of a window to change the size of the window. To change the size of the My Computer window, complete the following step.

Steps To Size a Window by Dragging

1 **Position the mouse pointer over the lower right corner of the My Computer window until the mouse pointer changes to a two-headed arrow. Drag the lower right corner upward and to the left until the window on your desktop resembles the window in Figure 1-27.**

As you drag the lower right corner, the My Computer window changes size and a vertical scroll bar displays (Figure 1-27). A **scroll bar** *is a bar that displays at the right edge and/or bottom edge of a window when the window contents are not completely visible. A vertical scroll bar contains an* **up scroll arrow**, *a* **down scroll arrow**, *and a* **scroll box**.

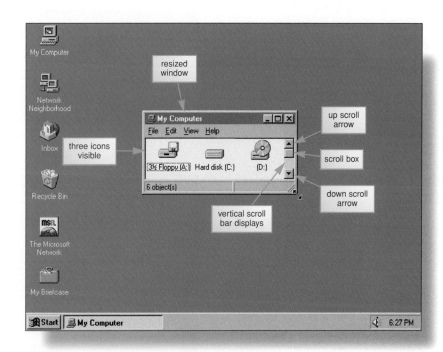

FIGURE 1-27

More *About*
Window Sizing

Windows 95 remembers the size of a window when you close the window. When you reopen the window, it will display in the same size as when you closed it.

The size of the scroll box in any window is dependent on the amount of the window that is not visible. The smaller the scroll box, the more of the window that is not visible. In addition to dragging a corner of a window, you can also drag any of the borders of a window.

Scrolling in a Window

You can use the scroll bar to view the contents of a window that are not visible. Scrolling can be accomplished in three ways: click the scroll arrows; click the scroll bar; and drag the scroll box.

To display the contents of the My Computer window by scrolling using scroll arrows, complete the steps on the next page.

More *About*
Scrolling

Most people will either maximize a window or size it so all the objects in the window are visible to avoid scrolling because scrolling takes time. It is more efficient not to have to scroll in a window.

Steps | To Scroll a Window Using Scroll Arrows

 1 **Point to the down scroll arrow on the vertical scroll bar.**

The mouse pointer points to the down scroll arrow on the scroll bar (Figure 1-28).

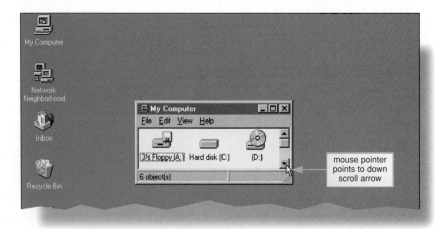

FIGURE 1-28

2 **Click the down scroll arrow one time.**

The window scrolls down (the icons move up in the window) and displays the tops of icons not previously visible (Figure 1-29). Because the window size does not change when you scroll, the contents of the window will change, as seen in the difference between Figure 1-28 and Figure 1-29.

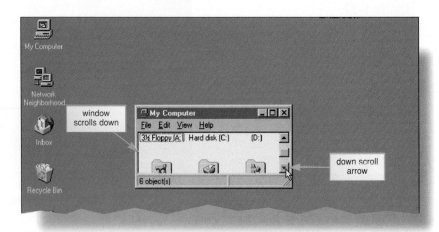

FIGURE 1-29

 3 **Click the down scroll arrow two more times.**

The scroll box moves to the bottom of the scroll bar and the icons in the last row of the window display (Figure 1-30).

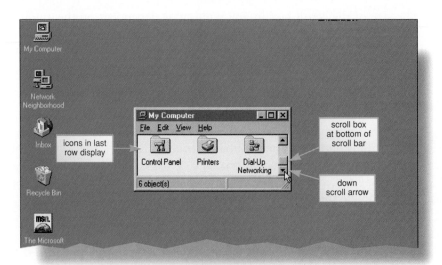

FIGURE 1-30

You can continuously scroll through a window using scroll arrows by clicking the up or down scroll arrow and holding down the left mouse button. The window continues to scroll until you release the left mouse button or you reach the top or bottom of the window.

You can also scroll by clicking the scroll bar itself. When you click the scroll bar, the window moves up or down a greater distance than when you click the scroll arrows.

A third way in which you can scroll through a window to view the window's contents is by dragging the scroll box. When you drag the scroll box, the window moves up or down as you drag.

Being able to view the contents of a window by scrolling is an important Windows 95 skill because the entire contents of a window may not be visible.

Resizing a Window

You might want to return a window to its original size. To return the My Computer window to about its original size, complete the following steps.

TO RESIZE A WINDOW

Step 1: Position the mouse pointer over the lower right corner of the My Computer window border until the mouse pointer changes to a two-headed arrow.
Step 2: Drag the lower right corner of the My Computer window until the window is the same size as shown in Figure 1-26 on page WIN 1.18, and then release the mouse button.

The My Computer window is about the same size as before you changed it.

Closing a Window

After you have completed your work in a window, normally you will close the window. To close the My Computer window, complete the following steps.

TO CLOSE A WINDOW

Step 1: Point to the Close button on the right of the title bar in the My Computer window.
Step 2: Click the Close button.

The My Computer window closes and the desktop contains no open windows.

Right-Drag

Right-drag means you point to an item, hold down the right mouse button, move the item to the desired location, and then release the right mouse button. When you right-drag an object, a context-sensitive menu displays. The context-sensitive menu contains commands specifically for use with the object being dragged. To right-drag the My Briefcase icon to the center of the desktop, perform the steps on the next page. If the My Briefcase icon does not display on your desktop, you will be unable to perform Step 1 through Step 3 on the next page.

◆ More *About* the Scroll Bar

In many application programs, clicking the scroll bar will move the window a full screen's worth of information up or down. You can step through a word processing document screen by screen, for example, by clicking the scroll bar.

◆ More *About* the Scroll Box

Dragging the scroll box is the most efficient technique to scroll long distances. In many application programs, such as Microsoft Word 7, as you scroll using the scroll box, the page number of the document displays next to the scroll box.

◆ More *About* Scrolling Guidelines

General scrolling guidelines: (1) To scroll short distances (line by line), click the scroll arrows; (2) To scroll one screen at a time, click the scroll bar; (3) To scroll long distances, drag the scroll box.

Steps To Right-Drag

1 **Point to the My Briefcase icon on the desktop, hold down the right mouse button, drag the icon diagonally toward the center of the desktop, and then release the right mouse button.**

The dragged My Briefcase ghosted icon and a context-sensitive menu display in the center of the desktop (Figure 1-31). The My Briefcase icon remains at its original location on the left of the screen. The context-sensitive menu contains four commands: Move Here, Copy Here, Create Shortcut(s) Here, and Cancel. The Move Here command in bold (dark) type identifies what happens if you were to drag the My Briefcase icon with the left mouse button.

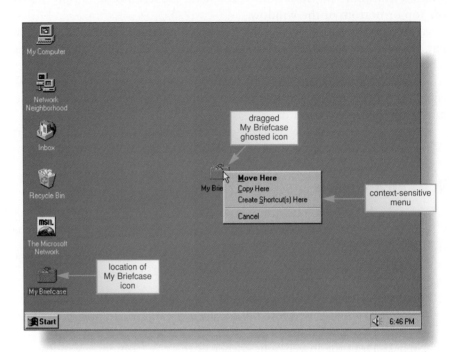

FIGURE 1-31

2 **Point to Cancel on the context-sensitive menu.**

The mouse pointer points to Cancel on the context-sensitive menu (Figure 1-32). The Cancel command is highlighted.

3 **Click Cancel on the context-sensitive menu.**

The context-sensitive menu and the dragged My Briefcase icon disappear from the screen.

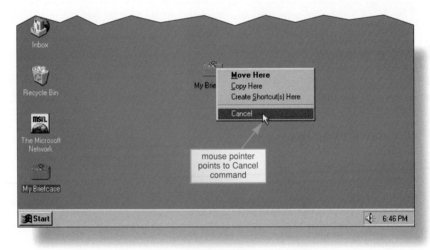

FIGURE 1-32

More About
Right-Dragging

Right-dragging was not even available on earlier versions of Windows, so you might find people familiar with Windows not even considering right-dragging. Because it always produces a context-sensitive menu, however, right-dragging is the safest way to drag.

Whenever you begin an operation but do not want to complete the operation, click Cancel on a context-sensitive menu or click the Cancel button in a dialog box. The Cancel command will reset anything you have done.

If you click Move Here on the context-sensitive menu shown in Figure 1-31, Windows 95 will move the icon from its current location to the new location. If you click the Copy Here command, the icon will be copied to the new location and two icons will display on the desktop. Windows 95 automatically will give the second icon and the associated file a different name. If you click the Create Shortcut(s) Here command, a special object called a shortcut will be created.

Although you can move icons by dragging with the primary (left) mouse button and by right-dragging with the secondary (right) mouse button, it is strongly suggested you right-drag because a menu displays and you can specify the exact operation you want to occur. When you drag using the left mouse button, a default operation takes place and the operation may not do what you want.

The Keyboard and Keyboard Shortcuts

FIGURE 1-33a

The **keyboard** is an input device on which you manually key, or type, data. Figure 1-33a shows the enhanced IBM 101-key keyboard and Figure 1-33b shows a Microsoft keyboard designed specifically for use with Windows 95. Many tasks you accomplish with a mouse also can be accomplished using a keyboard.

To perform tasks using the keyboard, you must understand the notation used to identify which keys to press. This notation is used throughout Windows 95 to identify **keyboard shortcuts**.

Keyboard shortcuts consist of: (1) pressing a single key (example: press F1); or, (2) holding down one key and pressing a second key, as shown by two key names separated with a plus sign (example: press CTRL+ESC). For example, to obtain Help about Windows 95, you can press the F1 key. To open the Start menu, hold down the CTRL key and press the ESC key (press CTRL+ESC).

Often, computer users will use keyboard shortcuts for operations they perform frequently. For example, many users find pressing the F1 key to start

FIGURE 1-33b

Windows 95 Help easier than using the Start menu as shown later in this project. As a user, you will likely find your own combination of keyboard and mouse operations that particularly suit you, but it is strongly recommended that generally you use the mouse.

Creating a Document by Starting an Application Program

A **program** is a set of computer instructions that carries out a task on your computer. An **application program** is a program that allows you to accomplish a specific task for which that program is designed. For example, a word processing program is an application program that allows you to create written documents, a spreadsheet program is an application program that allows you to create spreadsheets and charts, and a presentation graphics application program allows you to create graphic presentations for display on a computer or as slides.

More *About* the Microsoft Keyboard

The Microsoft keyboard in Figure 1-33(b) not only has special keys for Windows 95, but also is designed ergonomically so you type with your hands apart. It takes a little time to get used to, but several authors on the Shelly Cashman Series writing team report they type faster with more accuracy and less fatigue when using the keyboard.

More *About* Application Programs

Some application programs, such as Notepad, are part of Windows 95. Most application programs, however, such as Microsoft Office 95, Lotus SmartSuite 96, and others must be purchased separately from Windows 95.

The most common activity on a computer is to run an application program to accomplish tasks using the computer. You can start an application program by using the Start button on the taskbar.

To illustrate the use of an application program to create a written document, assume each morning you create a daily reminders list so you will remember the tasks you must accomplish throughout the day. You print the document containing the reminders for your use. On occasion, you must update the daily reminders list as events occur during the day. You have decided to use **Notepad**, a popular application program available with Windows 95, to create your list.

To create the list, one method you can use with Windows 95 is to start the Notepad application program using the Start button on the taskbar. After the Notepad program is started, you can enter your daily reminders.

To start the Notepad program, perform the following steps.

Steps To Start a Program

1 **Click the Start button on the taskbar. Point to Programs on the Start menu. Point to Accessories on the Programs submenu. If you happen to point to another command on one of the menus or submenus, a different submenu might display. Merely move the mouse so it points to Programs and then Accessories to display the correct menu and submenus.**

Windows 95 opens the Start menu, the Programs submenu, and the Accessories submenu (Figure 1-34). The mouse pointer points to Accessories on the Programs submenu. The Accessories submenu contains the Notepad command to start the Notepad program. Notice that whenever you point to a menu name that has a right arrow following it, a submenu displays. You might find more, fewer, or different commands on the submenus on your computer.

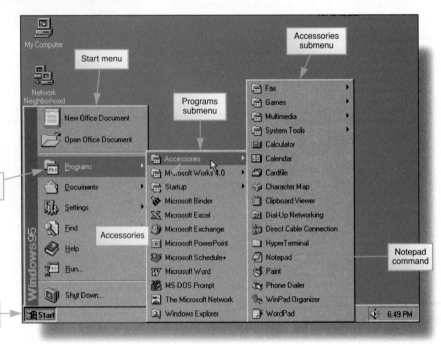

FIGURE 1-34

2 **Point to Notepad on the Accessories submenu.**

When the mouse pointer points to Notepad on the Accessories submenu, the Notepad command is highlighted (Figure 1-35).

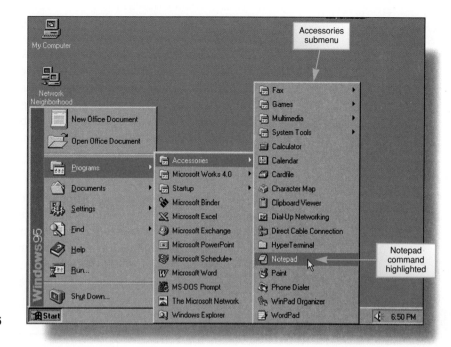

FIGURE 1-35

3 **Click Notepad.**

*Windows 95 starts the Notepad program by opening the Notepad window on the desktop and adding an indented Notepad button to the taskbar (Figure 1-36). Notepad is the active window (dark blue title bar). The word Untitled in the window title (Untitled - Notepad) and on the Notepad button indicates the document has not been saved on disk. The menu bar contains the following menu names: File, Edit, Search, and Help. The area below the menu bar contains an insertion point and two scroll bars. The **insertion point** is a flashing vertical line that indicates the point at which text typed on the keyboard will be displayed. The scroll bars do not contain scroll boxes, indicating the document is not large enough to allow scrolling.*

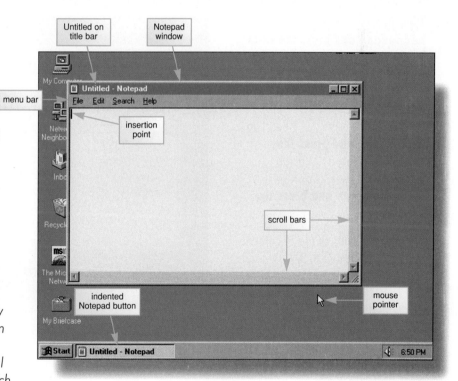

FIGURE 1-36

> ▶**Other**Ways
>
> 1. Right-click desktop, point to New, click Text Document, double-click the New Text Document icon
> 2. Click Start button, click Run, type Notepad, click OK button
> 3. Press CTRL+ESC, press R, type Notepad, press ENTER key

After you have started an application program such as Notepad, you can use the program to prepare your document.

Windows 95 provides a number of ways in which to accomplish a particular task. When a task is illustrated by a series of steps in this book, those steps may not be the only way in which the task can be done. If you can accomplish the same task using other methods, the Other Ways box specifies the other methods. In each case, the method shown in the steps is the preferred method, but it is important you are aware of all the techniques you can use.

Creating a Document

To create a document in Notepad, you must type the text you want in the document. After typing a line of text, press the ENTER key to indicate the end of the line. If you press the ENTER key when the insertion point is on a line by itself, Notepad inserts a blank line in the document. To create the Daily Reminders document, perform the following step.

Steps **To Create a Document**

1 **Type** Daily Reminders - Wednesday **and press the ENTER key twice. Type** 1. Call Tim Hoyle - Photoshop retouch due **and press the ENTER key. Type** 2. Memo to Linda Tomms - Meeting next week **and press the ENTER key. Type** 3. Lunch with Harris - Noon, Remmington's **and press the ENTER key.**

The first five lines of the document are entered (Figure 1-37). A blank line is inserted following the first line. The insertion point is positioned on the sixth line of the document.

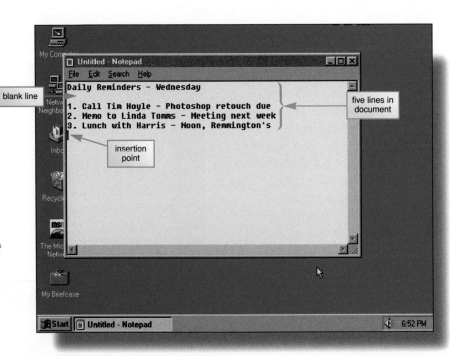

FIGURE 1-37

More *About*
Saving a Document

Most people who have used a computer can tell at least one horror story of working on their computer for a long stretch of time and then losing the work because of some malfunction with the computer or even with the operating system or application program. Be Warned: Save and save often to protect the work you have completed on your computer.

Saving a Document on Disk

When you create a document using a program such as Notepad, the document is stored in the main memory (RAM) of your computer. If you close the program without saving the document or if your computer accidentally loses electrical power, the document will be lost. To protect against the accidental loss of a document and to allow you to easily modify the document in the future, you can save the document on disk.

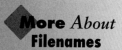
When you save a document, you must assign a filename to the document. All documents are identified by a filename. Typical filenames are Daily Reminders - Wednesday, Mileage Log, and Automobile Maintenance. A filename can contain up to 255 characters, including spaces. Any uppercase or lowercase character is valid when creating a filename, except a backslash (\), slash (/), colon (:), asterisk (*), question mark (?), quotation mark ("), less than symbol (<), greater than symbol (>), or vertical bar (|). Filenames cannot be CON, AUX, COM1, COM2, COM3, COM4, LPT1, LPT2, LPT3, PRN, or NUL.

To associate a document with an application, Windows 95 assigns an extension of a period and up to three characters to each document. All documents created using the Notepad program, which are text documents, are saved with the .TXT extension. To save the document you created using Notepad on a floppy disk in drive A of your computer using the filename, Daily Reminders - Wednesday, perform the following steps.

◆ **More** *About* **Filenames**

Because of restrictions with Microsoft DOS, previous versions of Windows allowed filenames of only eight or fewer characters. F56QPSLA, and similar indecipherable names, were common. Microsoft touts the long filename capability of Windows 95 as a significant breakthrough. Apple Macintosh users, however, shrug and ask what's the big deal. They have used long filenames for years.

Steps **To Save a Document on Disk**

① **Insert a formatted floppy disk into drive A on your computer. Click File on the menu bar.**

Windows 95 highlights the File menu name on the menu bar and opens the File menu in the Notepad window (Figure 1-38). The mouse pointer points to File on the menu bar.

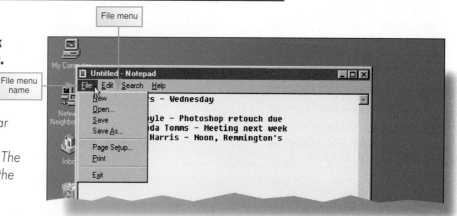

FIGURE 1-38

② **Point to Save As on the File menu.**

The mouse pointer points to the Save As command on the File menu (Figure 1-39). The ellipsis (...) following the Save As command indicates Windows 95 requires more information to carry out the Save As command and will open a dialog box when you click Save As. A **dialog box** *displays whenever Windows 95 needs to supply information to you or wants you to enter information or select among several options.*

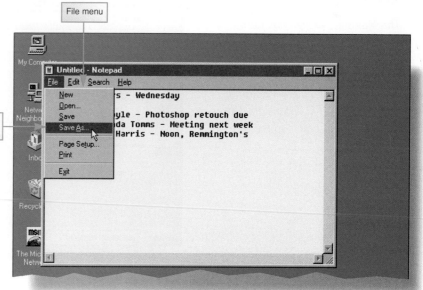

FIGURE 1-39

3 Click Save As.

*Windows 95 displays the Save As dialog box (Figure 1-40). The Save As dialog box becomes the active window (dark blue title bar) and the Notepad window becomes the **inactive window** (light blue title bar). The Save As dialog box contains the Save in drop-down list box. A **drop-down list box** is a rectangular box containing text and a down arrow on the right. The Save in drop-down list box displays the Desktop icon and Desktop name. The entry in the Save in drop-down list box indicates where the file will be stored. At the bottom of the dialog box is the File name text box. A **text box** is a rectangular area in which you can enter text. The File name text box contains the highlighted entry, Untitled. When you type the filename from the keyboard, the filename will replace the highlighted entry in the File name text box.*

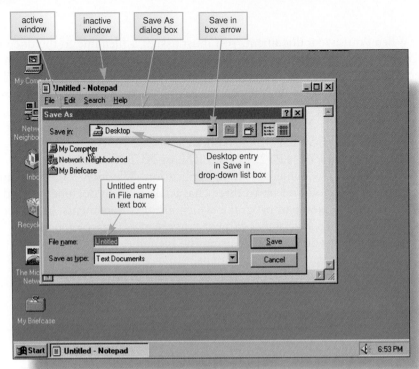

FIGURE 1-40

4 Type Daily Reminders - Wednesday **in the File name text box. Point to the Save in box arrow.**

The filename, Daily Reminders – Wednesday, and an insertion point display in the File name text box (Figure 1-41). When you save this document, Notepad will automatically add the .TXT extension. The mouse pointer points to the Save in box arrow.

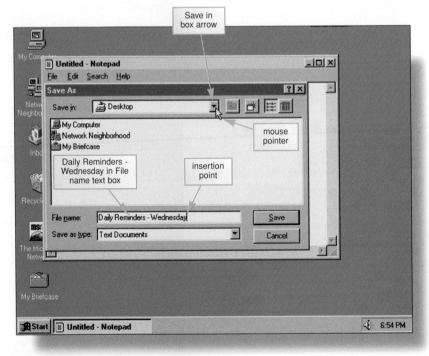

FIGURE 1-41

5 Click the Save in box arrow and then point to the 3½ Floppy [A:] icon.

Windows 95 displays the Save in drop-down list (Figure 1-42). The list contains various elements of your computer, including the Desktop, My Computer, Network Neighborhood, and My Briefcase. Within My Computer are 3½ Floppy [A:], Hard disk [C:], and [D:]. When you point to the 3½ Floppy [A:] icon, the entry in the list is highlighted.

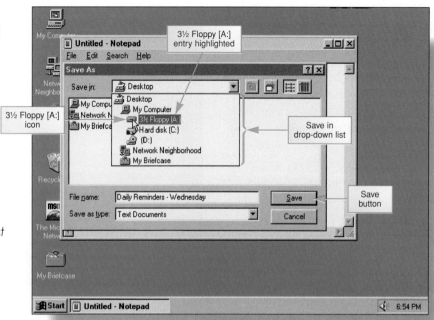

FIGURE 1-42

6 Click the 3½ Floppy [A:] icon and then point to the Save button.

The 3½ Floppy [A:] entry displays in the Save in drop-down list box (Figure 1-43). This specifies that the file will be saved on the floppy disk in drive A using the filename specified in the File name text box. The mouse pointer points to the Save button.

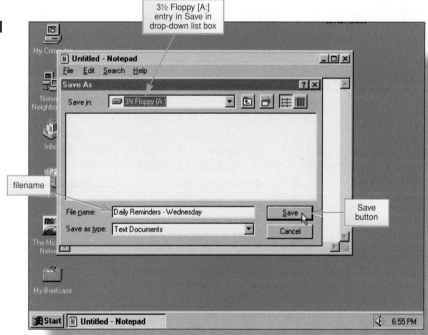

FIGURE 1-43

7 **Click the Save button.**

*Windows 95 displays an **hourglass icon** while saving the Daily Reminders - Wednesday document on the floppy disk in drive A, closes the Save As dialog box, makes the Notepad window the active window, and inserts the filename on the Notepad window title bar and on the button on the taskbar (Figure 1-44). The filename on the title bar may or may not display the .TXT extension, depending on the setting on your computer. The hourglass icon indicates Windows 95 requires a brief interval of time to save the document. The filename on the button on the taskbar (Daily Reminders - We...) contains an ellipsis to indicate the entire button name does not fit on the button. To display the entire button name for a button on the taskbar, point to the button.*

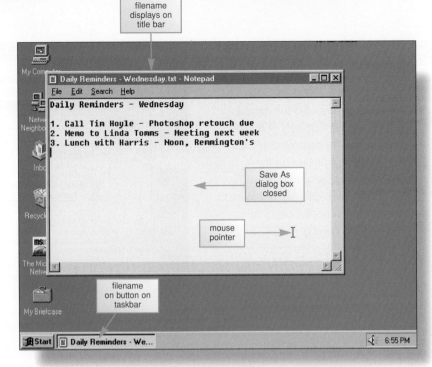

FIGURE 1-44

OtherWays

1. On File menu click Save, type filename, select drive and folder, click Save button
2. Press ALT+F, press A, type filename, select drive and folder, press S

The method shown in the previous steps for saving a file on a floppy disk can be used to save a file on a hard disk, such as drive C, or even on the desktop.

In Figure 1-38 on page WIN 1.27, the File menu displays. Once you have opened a menu on the menu bar, you need merely point to another menu name on the menu bar to open that menu. Thus, in Figure 1-38, if you point to Edit on the menu bar, the Edit menu will display. If you accidentally move the mouse pointer off the menu you want to display, point back to the menu name to display the desired menu. To close a menu without carrying out a command, click anywhere on the desktop except on the menu.

Printing a Document

Quite often, after creating a document and saving it, you will want to print it. Printing can be accomplished directly from an application program. To print the Daily Reminders – Wednesday document, perform the following steps.

More *About* **Printing**

Printing is and will remain important for documents. Many sophisticated application programs, however, are extending the printing capability to include transmitting faxes, sending e-mail, and even posting documents on Web pages of the World Wide Web.

Steps **To Print a Document**

1 Click File on the menu bar and then point to Print on the File menu.

The File menu displays and the mouse pointer points to the Print command (Figure 1-45). As with all menu commands when you point to them, the Print command is highlighted.

FIGURE 1-45

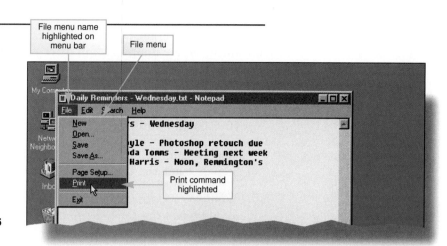

2 Click Print.

A Notepad dialog box briefly displays with a message that indicates the Daily Reminders document is being printed (Figure 1-46). The dialog box disappears after the report has been printed. To cancel printing, you can click the Cancel button. The printed report is shown in Figure 1-47. Notepad automatically places the filename at the top of the page and a page number at the bottom of the page.

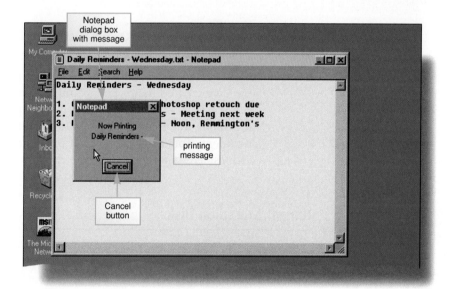

FIGURE 1-46

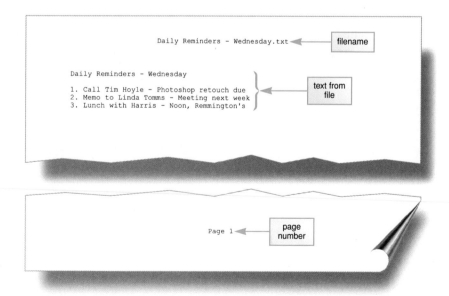

FIGURE 1-47

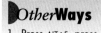

Closing a Program

After creating the Daily Reminders – Wednesday document, saving the document on the floppy disk in drive A, and printing it, your use of the Notepad program is complete. Therefore, the Notepad program should be closed by performing the following steps.

Other Ways

1. Double-click Notepad logo on title bar
2. On File menu click Exit
3. Press ALT+F4

TO CLOSE A PROGRAM

Step 1: Point to the Close button on the Notepad title bar.
Step 2: Click the Close button.

Windows 95 closes the Daily Reminders – Wednesday.txt – Notepad window and removes the Daily Reminders – Wednesday.txt – Notepad button from the taskbar.

Modifying a Document Stored on Disk

Many documents you create will need to be modified at some point in time after you have created them. For example, the Daily Reminders - Wednesday document should be modified each time you determine another task to be done. To modify an existing document, you can start the application program and open the document. To start the Notepad program and open the Daily Reminders – Wednesday document, complete the following steps.

Steps **To Open a Document Stored on Disk**

① **Click the Start button on the taskbar. Point to Programs. Point to Accessories. Point to Notepad.**

The Start menu, Programs sub-menu, and Accessories submenu display (Figure 1-48). The mouse pointer points to the Notepad command.

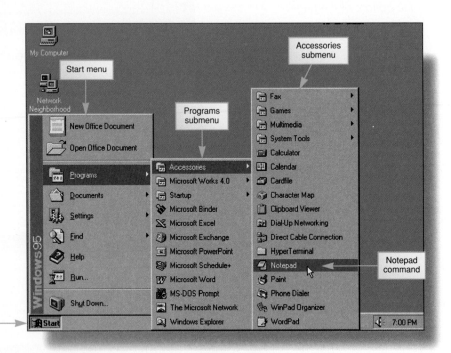

FIGURE 1-48

2 Click Notepad. When the Notepad window opens, click File on the menu bar and then point to Open on the File menu.

Windows 95 starts the Notepad program (Figure 1-49). The Untitled – Notepad button on the taskbar indicates no document has been opened. The File menu displays and the mouse pointer points to the Open command.

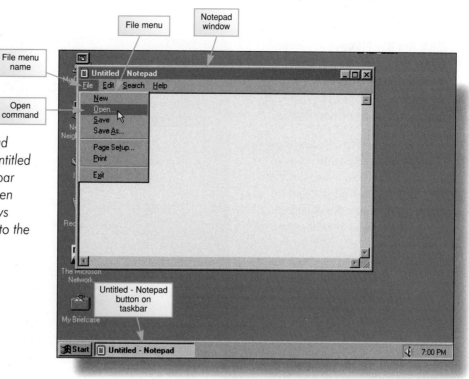

FIGURE 1-49

3 Click Open. Click the Look in box arrow. Point to the 3½ Floppy [A:] icon.

Windows 95 displays the Open dialog box (Figure 1-50). When you click the Look in box arrow, the Look in drop-down list displays. The mouse pointer points to the 3½ Floppy [A:] icon. The 3½ Floppy [A:] entry is highlighted.

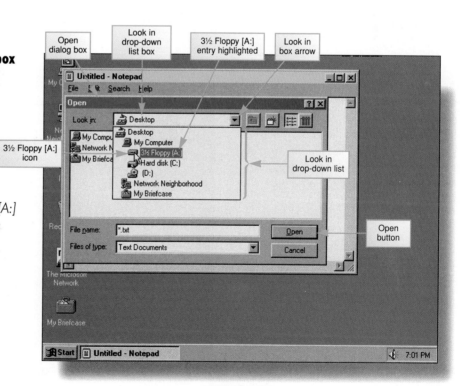

FIGURE 1-50

4 **Click the 3½ Floppy [A:] icon. When the filenames display in the window, click Daily Reminders – Wednesday.txt and then point to the Open button.**

Windows 95 places the 3½ Floppy [A:] icon and entry in the Look in drop-down list box, indicating that the file to be opened is found on the floppy disk in drive A (Figure 1-51). The names of folders and/or text document files stored on the floppy disk in drive A are displayed in the window below the Look in drop-down list box. The Daily Reminders - Wednesday.txt file is selected, as indicated by the high-light, and the mouse pointer points to the Open button. Notice that the Daily Reminders – Wednesday.txt filename displays in the File name text box, indicating this is the file that will be opened.

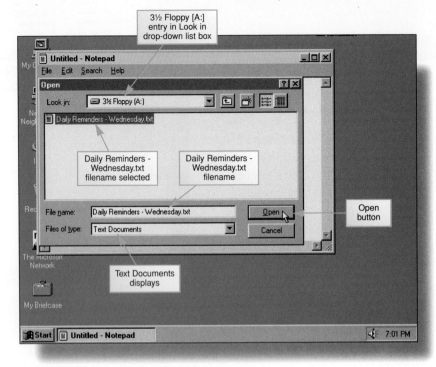

FIGURE 1-51

5 **Click the Open button.**

Windows 95 opens the Daily Reminders – Wednesday.txt file and displays it in the Notepad window (Figure 1-52). The filename displays on the title bar of the Notepad window and on the button on the taskbar.

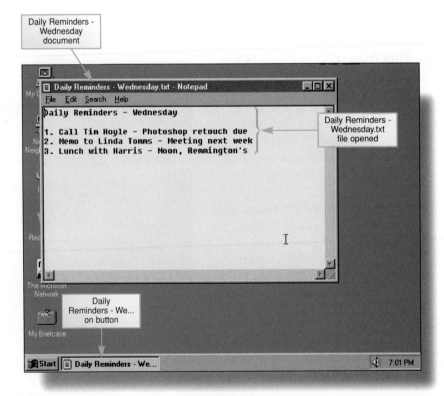

FIGURE 1-52

OtherWays

1. Double-click My Computer icon, double-click drive A icon, double-click file icon

2. Press ALT+F, press O, select drive and folder, type file-name, press O

After opening the Daily Reminders – Wednesday document, perform the following step to modify the document by adding another line.

TO MODIFY A DOCUMENT

Step 1: Press the DOWN ARROW key five times, type 4. E-Mail Sue Wells -
Adobe Illustrator drawing as the new line, and then press the
ENTER key.

After modifying the Daily Reminders – Wednesday document, you should
save the modified document on the floppy disk in drive A using the same filename. To save the modified document on the disk, complete the following steps.

Steps To Save a Modified Document on Disk

1 **Click File on the menu bar and
then point to Save.**

*The File menu opens and
the mouse pointer points
to the Save command
(Figure 1-53). The Save command
is used to save a file that has
already been created.*

2 **Click Save.**

*The modified document is stored
on the floppy disk in drive A and
the Notepad window remains
open. Whenever you use the Save
command, the document is stored
using the same filename in the
same location from which it was
opened.*

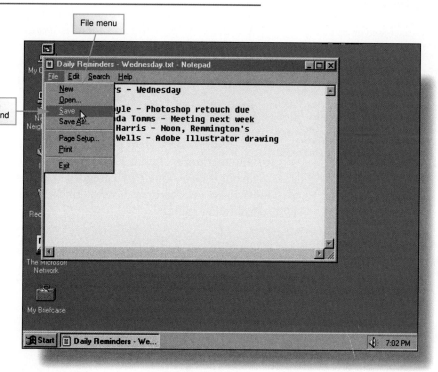

FIGURE 1-53

If you want to print the modified document, click File on the menu bar and
then click Print on the File menu in the same manner as shown in Figure 1-45 and
Figure 1-46 on page WIN 1.31.

Closing the Notepad Program

After modifying the document and storing the modified document on the
floppy disk in drive A, normally you will close the Notepad program. To close the
Notepad program, complete the step on the next page.

WINDOWS 95 TIPS
• You can close the
Notepad program by
double-clicking the icon to
the left of the window title
on the title bar.

LECTURE NOTES
• Emphasize that
Windows Help is available
for Windows 95 and all
applications running
under Windows 95.

More *About*
Windows 95 Help

If you purchased an operating
system or application program
five years ago, you received at
least one, and more often several, thick and heavy technical
manuals that explained the software. With Windows 95, you
receive a skinny manual less
than 100 pages in length. The
online Help feature of Windows
95 replaces reams and reams
of printed pages in hard-to-
understand technical manuals.

ILLUSTRATIONS
Figures 1-54 and 1-55

TO CLOSE A PROGRAM

Step 1: Click the Close button on the right of the Notepad title bar.

*The Notepad window closes and the Notepad button on the taskbar
disappears.*

Modifying an existing document is a common occurrence and should be well
understood when using Windows 95.

Using Windows Help

One of the more powerful application programs for use in Windows 95 is
Windows Help. Windows Help is available when using Windows 95, or when
using any application program running under Windows 95, to assist you in
using Windows 95 and the various application programs. It contains answers to
virtually any question you can ask with respect to Windows 95.

Contents Sheet

Windows 95 Help provides a variety of ways in which to obtain information.
One method to find a Help topic involves using the Contents sheet to browse
through Help topics by category. To illustrate this method, you will use Windows
95 Help to determine how to find a topic in Help. To start Help, complete the
following steps.

Steps **To Start Help**

1 **Click the Start button on the
taskbar. Point to Help on the
Start menu.**

*Windows 95 opens the Start
menu (Figure 1-54). Because the
mouse pointer points to the Help
command, the Help command is
highlighted.*

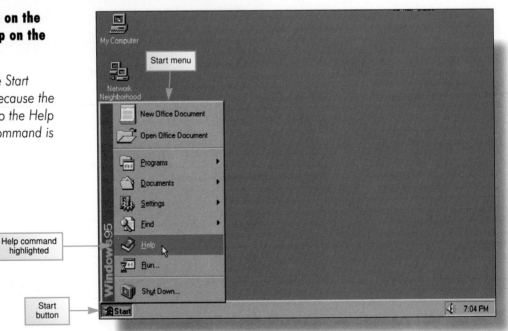

FIGURE 1-54

2 **Click Help on the Start menu. If the Contents sheet does not display, click the Contents tab.**

Windows 95 opens the Help Topics: Windows Help window (Figure 1-55). The window contains three **tabs** *(Contents, Index, and Find). The* **Contents sheet** *is visible in the window. Clicking either the Index tab or the Find tab opens the Index or Find sheet, respectively. The Contents sheet contains two* **Help topics** *preceded by a question mark icon and five books. Each book consists of a closed book icon followed by a book name. The first Help topic, Tour: Ten minutes to using Windows, is highlighted. Three command buttons (Display, Print, and Cancel) display at the bottom of the window.*

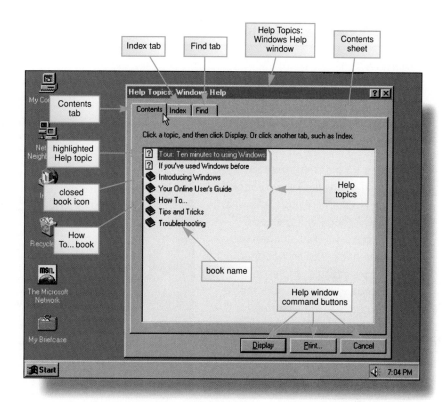

FIGURE 1-55

Other Ways

1. Press F1, press CTRL+TAB or CTRL+SHIFT+TAB to highlight desired sheet

In the Help window shown in Figure 1-55, the closed book icon indicates Help topics or more books are contained within the book. The question mark icon indicates a Help topic without any further subdivisions.

In addition to starting Help by using the Start button, you can also start Help by pressing the F1 key.

After starting Help, the next step is to find the topic in which you are interested. To find the topic that describes how to find a topic in Help, complete the steps on the next two pages.

Steps To Use Help to Find a Topic in Help

1 **Double-click How To... in the Help Topics: Windows Help window. Point to the Use Help closed book.**

Windows 95 highlights the How To book and opens the How To book (Figure 1-56). The ellipsis following the How To book indicates additional books will display when you open the book. The list of closed book icons indicates more Help information is available. The mouse pointer points to the Use Help closed book icon. The Close button in Figure 1-56 replaces the Display button in Figure 1-55. If you click the Close button, the How To book will close and the list of books below the How To book disappears.

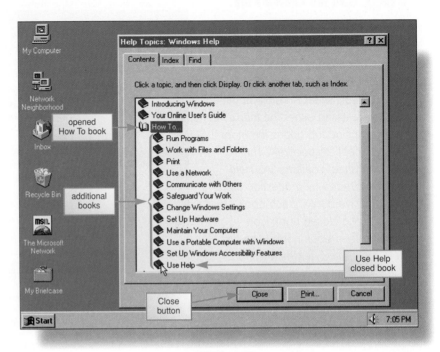

FIGURE 1-56

2 **Double-click the Use Help closed book icon and then point to Finding a topic in Help in the opened Use Help book.**

Windows 95 opens the Use Help book and displays several Help topics in the book (Figure 1-57). The mouse pointer points to Finding a topic in Help.

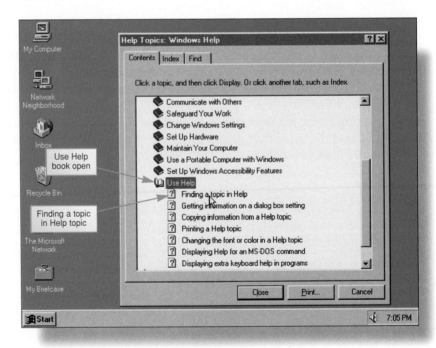

FIGURE 1-57

3 Double-click Finding a topic in Help.

Windows 95 closes the Help Topics: Windows Help window and opens the Windows Help window (Figure 1-58). The window contains three buttons (Help Topics, Back, and Options), steps to find a topic in Help, and a Tip. The Windows Help button displays on the taskbar.

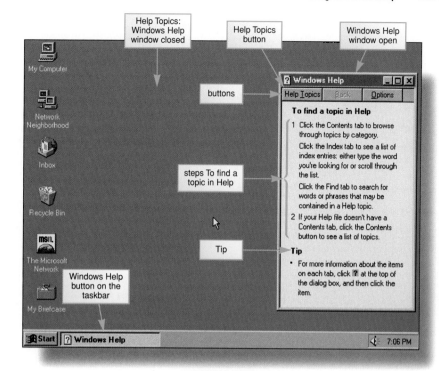

FIGURE 1-58

4 After reading the information in the Windows Help window, click the Help Topics button in the Windows Help window.

The Help Topics: Windows Help window displays together with the Windows Help window (Figure 1-59).

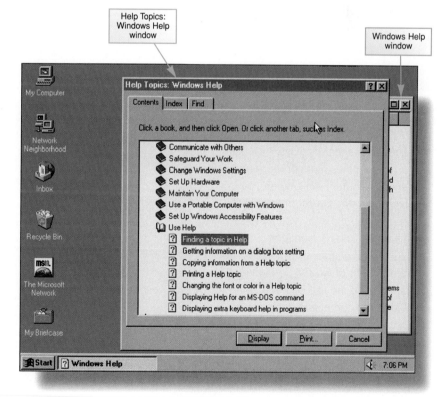

FIGURE 1-59

> ### OtherWays
>
> 1. Press DOWN ARROW until book or topic highlighted, press ENTER, continue until Help topic displays, read Help topic, press T

More *About* **the Index Sheet**

The Index sheet is probably the best source of information in Windows Help because you can enter the subject you are interested in. Sometimes, however, you will have to be creative to discover the index entry that answers your question because the most obvious entry will not always lead to your answer.

Clicking the Help Topics button in the Windows Help window will always display the Help Topics: Windows Help window.

In Figure 1-58 on the previous page, if you click the Back button in the Windows Help window (when the button is not dimmed), Windows 95 will display the previously displayed Help topic. Clicking the Options button in the Windows Help window allows you to annotate a Help topic, copy or print a Help topic, change the font and color scheme of Help windows, and control how Help windows display in relation to other windows on the desktop.

Notice also in Figure 1-58 that the Windows Help title bar contains a Minimize button, a Maximize button, and a Close button. You can minimize and maximize the Windows Help window, and you can also close the Windows Help window without returning to the Help Topics: Windows Help window.

Index Sheet

A second method to find answers to your questions about Windows 95 or application programs is the Index sheet. The **Index sheet** lists a large number of index entries, each of which references one or more Help screens. To learn more about Windows 95 basic skills by using the Index sheet, and to see an example of animation available with Help, complete the following steps.

Steps **To Use the Help Index Sheet**

1 **Click the Index tab. Type** basic skills **(the flashing insertion point is positioned in the text box). Point to the Display button.**

The Index sheet displays, including a list of entries that can be referenced (Figure 1-60). When you type an entry, the list automatically scrolls and the entry you type, such as basic skills, is highlighted. To see additional entries, use the scroll bar at the right of the list. To highlight an entry in the list, click the entry. On some computers, the basic skills entry may not be present. On those machines, select another topic of interest to you.

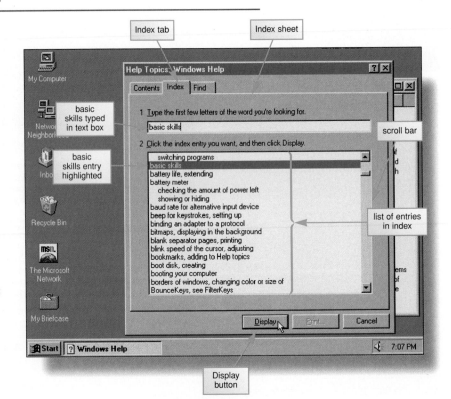

FIGURE 1-60

2 **Click the Display button. Click the Maximize button in the Windows Help title bar. Point to the Sizing windows button.**

The Windows Help window opens and a screen titled, The Basics, displays (Figure 1-61). The window is maximized and the Restore button displays in place of the Maximize button. The screen includes six buttons to learn Windows essentials and a picture of the Windows 95 desktop. When the mouse pointer is positioned on one of the buttons, it changes to a hand with a pointing finger. The Windows Help button displays on the taskbar.

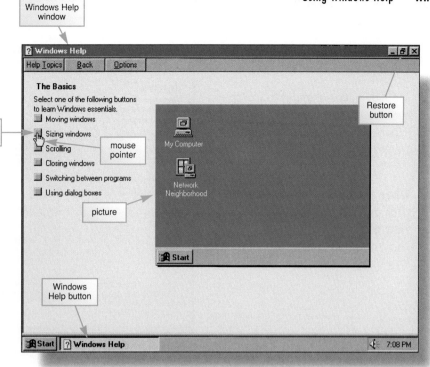

FIGURE 1-61

3 **Click the Sizing windows button. Point to the Play button (the button with the right arrow) below the picture on the right.**

The words, Sizing windows, display in bold, the My Computer window is added to the picture on the right, and the controls to play the animation display (Figure 1-62). The Play button will play the animation, the Option button displays a series of options regarding the animation, and the slide indicates progress when the animation plays. Text that explains how to accomplish the task, such as sizing windows, displays above the picture. On some computers, the animation might not be available. On those computers, instead of displaying the animation picture, the message, Unable to display graphic, will display on the screen. The text above the picture that explains how to perform the task still displays.

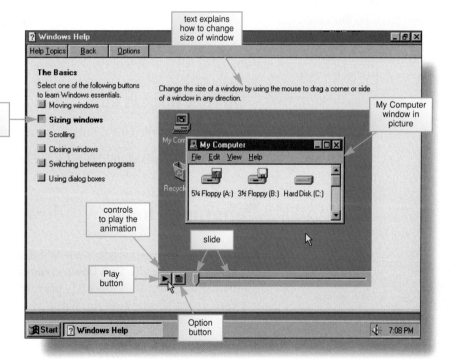

FIGURE 1-62

4 **Click the Play button if it displays on the screen.**

The Play button changes to a Stop button and the animation plays (Figure 1-63). The slide indicates the progress of the animation.

5 **When the animation is complete, click any buttons you wish to view other animations.**

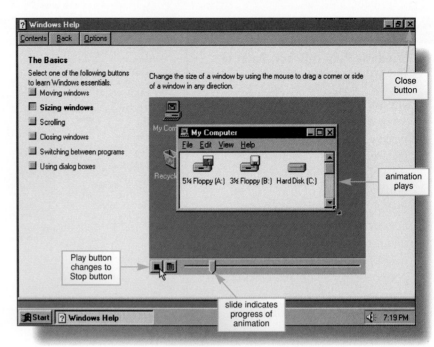

FIGURE 1-63

OtherWays

1. Press CTRL+TAB, type topic name, press ENTER, press ALT+SPACEBAR, press X, press TAB until topic highlighted, press ENTER, click Play button

After viewing Help topics, normally you will close Windows Help. To close Windows Help, complete the following step.

TO CLOSE WINDOWS HELP

Step 1: Click the Close button on the title bar of the Windows Help window.

Windows 95 closes the Windows Help window.

Shutting Down Windows 95

More *About* **Shut Down Procedures**

Some users of Windows 95 have turned off their computer without following the shut down procedure only to find data they thought they had stored on disk was lost. Because of the way Windows 95 writes data on the disk, it is important you shut down windows properly so you do not lose your work.

After completing your work with Windows 95, you might want to shut down Windows 95 using the **Shut Down command** on the Start menu. If you are sure you want to shut down Windows 95, perform the steps on the next page. If you are not sure about shutting down Windows 95, read the following steps without actually performing them.

Steps **To Shut Down Windows 95**

1 **Click the Start button on the taskbar and then point to Shut Down on the Start menu.**

Windows 95 displays the Start menu (Figure 1-64). The Shut Down command is highlighted because the mouse pointer points to it.

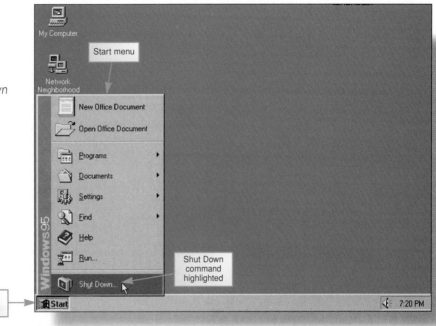

FIGURE 1-64

2 **Click Shut Down. Point to the Yes button in the Shut Down Windows dialog box.**

Windows 95 darkens the entire desktop and opens the Shut Down Windows dialog box (Figure 1-65). The dialog box contains four option buttons. The selected option button, Shut down the computer?, indicates that clicking the Yes button will shut down Windows 95.

3 **Click the Yes button.**

Two screens display while Windows 95 is shutting down. The first screen containing the text, Shutting down Windows, displays momentarily while Windows 95 is being shut down. Then, a second screen containing the text, It is okay to turn off your computer, displays. At this point you can to turn off your computer. When shutting down Windows 95, you should never turn off your computer before this last screen displays.

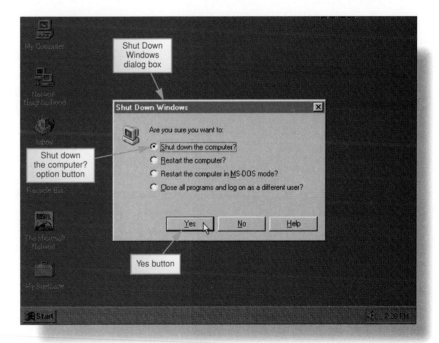

FIGURE 1-65

OtherWays

1. Press CTRL+ESC, press U, press UP ARROW or DOWN ARROW until option button selected, press ENTER

2. Press ALT+F4, press UP ARROW or DOWN ARROW until option button selected, press ENTER

If you accidentally click Shut Down on the Start menu and you do not want to shut down Windows 95, click the No button in the Shut Down Windows dialog box to return to normal Windows 95 operation.

Project Summary

Project 1 illustrated the Microsoft Windows 95 graphical user interface. You started Windows 95, learned the parts of the desktop, and learned to point, click, right-click, double-click, drag, and right-drag. You created a document by starting Notepad, entering text, saving the document on a floppy disk, and printing the document. You then modified the Notepad document and saved the modified document. Using both the Help Content and the Help Index sheets you obtained Help about Microsoft Windows 95. You shut down Windows 95 using the Shut Down command on the Start menu.

What You Should Know

Having completed this project, you should now be able to perform the following tasks:

▶ Close a Program *(WIN 1.32, WIN 1.36)*

▶ Close the Welcome Screen *(WIN 1.7)*

▶ Close a Window *(WIN 1.20)*

▶ Close a Window and Reopen a Window *(WIN 1.16)*

▶ Close Windows Help *(WIN 1.42)*

▶ Create a Document *(WIN 1.26)*

▶ Maximize and Restore a Window *(WIN 1.14)*

▶ Minimize and Redisplay a Window *(WIN 1.13)*

▶ Modify a Document *(WIN 1.35)*

▶ Move an Object by Dragging *(WIN 1.17)*

▶ Open a Document Stored on Disk *(WIN 1.32)*

▶ Open a Window by Double-Clicking *(WIN 1.12)*

▶ Point and Click *(WIN 1.9)*

▶ Print a Document *(WIN 1.31)*

▶ Resize a Window *(WIN 1.21)*

▶ Right-Click *(WIN 1.11)*

▶ Right-Drag *(WIN 1.22)*

▶ Save a Document on Disk *(WIN 1.27)*

▶ Save a Modified Document on Disk *(WIN 1.35)*

▶ Scroll a Window Using Scroll Arrows *(WIN 1.20)*

▶ Shut Down Windows 95 *(WIN 1.43)*

▶ Size a Window by Dragging *(WIN 1.19)*

▶ Start a Program *(WIN 1.24)*

▶ Start Help *(WIN 1.36)*

▶ Use Help to Find a Topic in Help *(WIN 1.38)*

▶ Use the Help Index Sheet *(WIN 1.40)*

Test Your Knowledge

1 True/False

Instructions: Circle T if the statement is true or F if the statement is false.

T F   1. A user interface is a combination of computer hardware and computer software.

T F   2. Click means press the right mouse button.

T F   3. When you drag an object on the desktop, Windows 95 displays a context-sensitive menu.

T F   4. You can resize a window by dragging the title bar of the window.

T F   5. Daily Reminders - Friday and Mileage Log are valid filenames.

T F   6. To save a new document created using Notepad, click Save As on the File menu.

T F   7. To print a document, click Print on the File menu.

T F   8. To open a document stored on a floppy disk, click Open on the Start menu.

T F   9. You can start Help by clicking the Start button and then clicking Help on the Start menu.

T F 10. To find an item in the Windows Help Index, type the first few characters of the item in the text box on the Contents sheet.

2 Multiple Choice

Instructions: Circle the correct response.

1. Through a user interface, the user is able to _____.
   a. control the computer
   b. request information from the computer
   c. respond to messages displayed by the computer
   d. all of the above

2. A context-sensitive menu opens when you _____ a(n) _____.
   a. right-click, object
   b. click, menu name on the menu bar
   c. click, submenu
   d. double-click, indented button on the taskbar

3. In this book, a dark blue title bar and an indented button on the taskbar indicate a window is _____.
   a. inactive
   b. minimized
   c. closed
   d. active

4. To view contents of a window that are not currently visible in the window, use the _____.
   a. title bar
   b. scroll bar
   c. menu bar
   d. Restore button

(continued)

A+ Test Your Knowledge

Multiple Choice *(continued)*

5. _____ is holding down the right mouse button, moving an item to the desired location, and then releasing the right mouse button.
   a. Double-clicking
   b. Right-clicking
   c. Right-dragging
   d. Pointing

6. The Notepad command used to start the Notepad application program is located on the _____ (sub)menu.
   a. Start
   b. Accessories
   c. Programs
   d. Help

7. To quit the Notepad application and close its window, _____.
   a. click the Close button on the Notepad title bar
   b. click File on the menu bar
   c. double-click the Notepad title bar
   d. click the Minimize button on the Notepad title bar

8. To save a Notepad document after modifying the document, _____.
   a. click the Close button on the Notepad title bar
   b. click the Minimize button on the Notepad title bar
   c. click Save on the File menu
   d. click Exit on the File menu

9. For information about an item on the Index sheet of the Help Topics: Windows Help window, _____.
   a. press the F1 key
   b. click the Question Mark button in the top right corner of the dialog box and then click the item
   c. click the Find tab in the Help Topics: Windows Help window
   d. press CTRL+F3

10. To shut down Windows 95, _____.
   a. click the Start button, click Shut Down on the Start menu, click the Shut down the computer? option button, and then click the Yes button
   b. click the Shut Down button on the Windows 95 File menu
   c. click the taskbar, click Close down Windows 95, and then click the Yes button
   d. press the F10 key and then click the Yes button

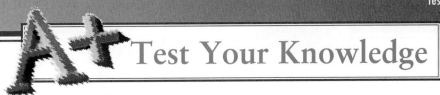

3 Identifying Objects on the Desktop

Instructions: On the desktop in Figure 1-66, arrows point to several items or objects on the desktop. Identify the items or objects in the spaces provided.

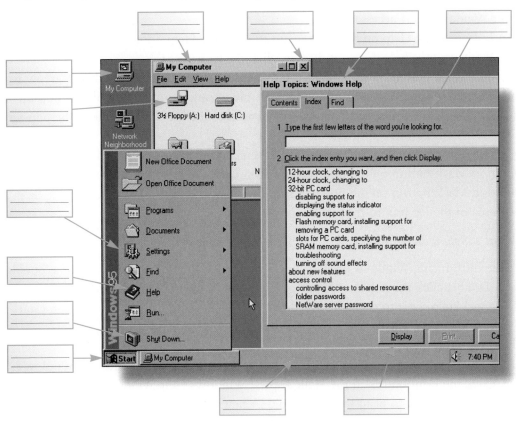

FIGURE 1-66

4 Saving a Document

Instructions: List the steps in the spaces provided to save a new Notepad file on a floppy disk in drive A using the filename, This is my file.

Step 1: _____

Step 2: _____

Step 3: _____

Step 4: _____

Step 5: _____

Step 6: _____

Step 7: _____

Use Help

1 Using Windows Help

Instructions: Use Windows Help and a computer to perform the following tasks.

Part 1: *Using the Question Mark Button*

1. Start Microsoft Windows 95 if necessary.
2. Click the Start button. Click Help on the Start menu to open the Help Topics: Windows Help window. If the Contents tab sheet does not display, click the Contents tab.
3. Click the Question Mark button on the title bar. The mouse pointer changes to a block arrow with question mark pointer. Click the list box containing the Help topics and Help books. A pop-up window explaining the list box displays. Click an open area of the list box to remove the pop-up window.
4. Click the Question Mark button on the title bar and then click the Display button.
5. Click the Question Mark button on the title bar and then click the Print button.
6. Click the Question Mark button on the title bar and then click the Cancel button.
7. Click an open area of the list box to remove the pop-up window.

Part 2: *Finding What's New with Windows 95*

1. Double-click the Introducing Windows book to open the book. Double-click the Welcome book to open the book. Double-click the A List of What's New book to open the book. Double-click the A new look and feel Help topic to open the Windows Help window. Click the first button (Start button and taskbar) and read the contents of the What's New window.
2. Click the Close button in the What's New window.
3. Click the Help Topics button in the Windows Help window to open the Help Topics: Windows Help window. Click the Print button in the Help Topics: Windows Help window. Click the OK button in the Print dialog box to print the Help topic (A new look and feel).
4. Click the Help Topics button in the Windows Help window.
5. Double-click the Welcome book to close the book.

Part 3: *Learning About Getting Your Work Done*

1. Double-click the Getting Your Work Done book to open the book. Double-click the Saving your work Help topic. Click the Save button and read the pop-up window.
2. Click other items in the Save As dialog box and read the pop-up windows.
3. Click the Help Topics button in the Windows Help window to open the Help Topics: Windows Help window. Click the Print button in the Help Topics: Windows Help window. Click the OK button in the Print dialog box to print the Saving your work Help topic.
4. Click the Close buttons in the Windows Help windows to close the windows.

? Use Help

2 Using Windows Help to Obtain Help

Instructions: Use Windows Help and a computer to perform the following tasks.

1. Find Help about viewing the Welcome screen that displays when you start Windows 95 by looking in the Tips of the Day book within the Tips and Tricks book in the Help Topics: Windows Help window. Answer the following questions in the spaces provided.
   a. How can you open the Welcome screen? _____
   b. How can you see the list of tips in the Welcome screen? _____
   c. Open the Welcome screen. Cycle through the tips in the Welcome screen. How can you set your computer's clock? _____
   d. Click the What's New button in the Welcome screen. According to Help, how do you start a program? _____
   e. Close the Welcome screen. Click the Help Topics button in the Windows Help window.

2. Find Help about keyboard shortcuts by looking in the Keyboard Shortcuts book. Answer the following questions in the spaces provided.
   a. What keyboard shortcut is used to quit a program? _____
   b. What keyboard shortcut is used to display the Start menu? _____
   c. What keyboard shortcut is used to view the shortcut menu for a selected item? _____
   d. What keyboard shortcut is used to rename an item? _____
   e. What keyboard shortcut is used to open the Save in list box (drop-down list box)? _____
   f. Click the Help Topics button in the Windows Help window.

3. Find Help about Notepad by looking in the For Writing and Drawing book. Answer the following questions in the spaces provided.
   a. Can you create or edit a text file that requires formatting using Notepad? _____
   b. What size file can you create using Notepad? _____
   c. Which program can you use to create a larger file? _____
   d. What is the only format used by Notepad to store a file? _____

4. Find Help about the Internet by looking in the Welcome to the Information Highway book. Answer the following questions in the spaces provided.
   a. List one source of online information available on the Internet. _____
   b. How do you use The Microsoft Network to sign up for the Internet?
   c. Where else can you find information about connecting to the Internet? _____

5. Find Help about what to do if you have a problem starting Windows 95. The process of solving such a problem is called troubleshooting. Answer the following questions in the spaces provided.
   a. What size floppy disk do you need to create a startup disk? _____
   b. To start Windows in safe mode, what do you do when you see the message "Starting Windows 95?" _____

6. Answer the following questions in the spaces provided.
   a. List two ways you can get Help in a dialog box: _____; _____.
   b. How can you print information displayed in a Help pop-up window?
   _____

(continued)

Use Help

Use Help *(continued)*

7. You have been assigned to obtain information on software licensing. Answer the following questions, and find and print information from Windows Help that supports your answers.
   a. How is computer software protected by law?
   b. What is software piracy? Why should you be concerned?
   c. Can you use your own software on both your desktop and your laptop computers?
   d. How can you identify illegal software?
8. Close all open Windows Help windows.

In the Lab

1 Improving Your Mouse Skills

Instructions: Use a computer to perform the following tasks:

1. Start Microsoft Windows 95 if necessary.
2. Click the Start button on the taskbar, point to Programs on the Start menu, point to Accessories on the Programs submenu, point to Games on the Accessories submenu, and click Solitaire on the Games submenu.
3. Click the Maximize button in the Solitaire window.
4. Click Help on the Solitaire menu bar.
5. Click Help Topics on the Help menu.
6. If the Contents sheet does not display, click the Contents tab.
7. Review the How to play Solitaire and Scoring information Help topics on the Contents sheet.
8. After reviewing the topics, close all Help windows.
9. Play the game of Solitaire.
10. Click the Close button on the Solitaire title bar to close the game.

2 Starting an Application, Creating a Document, and Modifying a Document

Instructions: Perform the following steps to start the Notepad application and create and modify a document.

Part 1: *Creating a Document*

1. Start Microsoft Windows 95 if necessary.
2. Click the Start button. Point to Programs on the Start menu. Point to Accessories on the Programs submenu. Click Notepad on the Accessories submenu.

In the Lab

3. Enter the document shown in Figure 1-67 in the Notepad document.

4. Insert a formatted floppy disk in drive A of your computer.

5. Click File on the menu bar. Click Save As on the File menu.

6. Type Office Supplies Shopping List - Tuesday in the File name text box.

7. Click the Save in box arrow. Click the 3½ Floppy [A:] icon. Click the Save button.

8. Click File on the menu bar. Click Print on the File menu.

9. Click the Close button on the Notepad title bar.

10. If you are not completing Part 2 of this assignment, remove your floppy disk from drive A.

```
Office Supplies Shopping List - Tuesday

1. Staples
2. 2 boxes of copier paper
3. Toner for computer printer
4. Box of formatted floppy disks
```

FIGURE 1-67

Part 2: *Modifying a Document*

1. Click the Start button, point to Programs on the Start menu, point to Accessories on the Programs submenu, and then click Notepad on the Accessories submenu.

2. Click File on the menu bar and then click Open on the File menu. Click the Look in box arrow and then click the 3½ Floppy [A:] icon. Click Office Supplies Shopping List - Tuesday. Click the Open button.

3. Press the DOWN ARROW key six times. Type 5. Two boxes of black ink pens and then press the ENTER key.

4. Click File on the menu bar and then click Save on the File menu.

5. Click File on the menu bar and then click Print on the File menu.

6. Click the Close button on the Notepad title bar.

7. Remove the floppy disk from drive A of your computer.

3 Creating a Document

Instructions: As a student, you would like to give a copy of your daily schedule to your parents and friends so you can be contacted in an emergency. To do this, you want to create a document for each weekday (Monday through Friday). Each document will have an appropriate title and contain your daily school and personal schedule. Each course in the document will contain the start and finish time for the course, course number, course title, room number, and instructor name. Other entries for extracurricular activities, sporting events, or personal events also will be included in the documents. Print the five documents on the printer and follow directions from your instructor for turning in this assignment. Store the five documents on a floppy disk.

Cases and Places

200 MHz

The difficulty of these case studies varies:

▶ Case studies preceded by a single half moon are the least difficult. You can complete these case studies using your own computer or a computer in the lab.

▶▶ Case studies preceded by two half moons are more difficult. You must research the topic presented using the Internet, a library, or another resource, and then prepare a brief written report.

▶▶▶ Case studies preceded by three half moons are the most difficult. You must visit a store or business to obtain the necessary information, and then use it to create a brief written report.

1 ▶ Your employer is concerned that some people in the company are not putting enough thought into software purchases. She has prepared a list of steps she would like everyone to follow when acquiring software (Figure 1-68).

You have been asked to use WordPad to prepare a copy of this list that can be posted in every department. Use the concepts and techniques presented in this project to start WordPad and create, save, and print the document. After you have printed one copy of the document, try experimenting with different WordPad features to make the list more eye-catching. If you like your changes, save and print a revised copy of the document. If WordPad is not available on your machine, use Notepad.

Steps in Software Acquisition

1. *Summarize your requirements*
2. *Identify potential vendors*
3. *Evaluate alternative software packages*
4. *Make the purchase*

FIGURE 1-68

2 ▶ The local community center has asked you to teach an introductory class on Windows 95 to a group of adults with little previous computer experience. The center director has sent you a note about one of his concerns (Figure 1-69).

Think of two topics about which people in the class may have questions. Use online Help to find answers to the questions. Consider how you would find answers to the same questions using a book. Write a response to the center director describing the advantages and disadvantages of using online Help instead of a book. Explain why you feel the class does or does not need a resource book. To make the director aware of online Help's limitations, tell how you think Microsoft could improve Help in Windows 95.

Is online Help enough for this group?

These people are pretty traditional and are used to having a printed text. Do we need to buy some kind of "help resource book" for everyone? We don't have much money, but on the other hand we don't want people to be disappointed.

Please think about it and get back to me.

FIGURE 1-69

Cases and Places

3 ▶▶ Early personal computer operating systems were adequate, but they were not user-friendly and had few advanced features. Over the past several years, however, personal computer operating systems have become increasingly easy to use, and some now offer features once available only on mainframe computers. Using the Internet, a library, or other research facility, write a brief report on four personal computer operating systems. Describe the systems, pointing out their similarities and differences. Discuss the advantages and disadvantages of each. Finally, tell which operating system you would purchase for your personal computer and explain why.

4 ▶▶ Many feel that Windows 95 was one of the most heavily promoted products ever released. Using the Internet, current computer magazines, or other resources, prepare a brief report on the background of Windows 95. Explain why Windows 95 was two years behind schedule and how it was promoted. Discuss the ways in which Windows 95 is different from earlier versions of Windows (such as Windows 3.1). Based on reviews of the new operating system, describe what people like and do not like about Windows 95. Finally, from what you have learned and your own experience, explain how you think Windows 95 could be improved.

5 ▶▶▶ Software must be compatible with (able to work with) the operating system of the computer on which it will be used. Visit a software vendor and find the five application packages (word processing programs, spreadsheet programs, games, and so on) you would most like to have. List the names of the packages and the operating system used by each. Make a second list of five similar packages that are compatible (meaning they use the same operating system). Using your two lists, write a brief report on how the need to purchase compatible software can affect buying application packages and even the choice of an operating system.

6 ▶▶▶ Because of the many important tasks it performs, most businesses put a great deal of thought into choosing an operating system for their personal computers. Interview people at a local business on the operating system they use with their personal computers. Based on your interviews, write a brief report on why the business chose that operating system, how satisfied they are with it, and under what circumstances they might consider switching to a different operating system.

7 ▶▶▶ In a recent television commercial from Apple Computers, a frustrated father tries to use Windows 95 to display pictures of dinosaurs for his young son. After waiting impatiently, the boy tells his father he is going next door to the neighbor's because they have a Mac. Visit a computer vendor and try an operating system with a graphical user interface other than Windows 95, such as Macintosh System 7.5 or OS/2. Write a brief report comparing the operating system to Windows 95, and explain which operating system you would prefer to have on your personal computer.

Putting the Squeeze on DATA

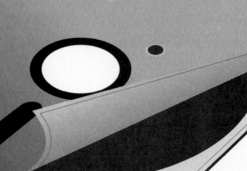

1978

320K

In 1994, a federal district court ruled that Microsoft violated the rights of Stac Electronics in the data compression software component of MS-DOS 6.2, Microsoft's operating system. In response, Microsoft paid Stac a royalty of $43 million and replaced MS-DOS 6.2 with version 6.21, which did not contain the offending code.

Why the lawsuit? Data compression software, which allows you to store more data on your hard disk, is an important component of your computer's software and is so valuable to its developers that they will sue to protect their rights.

Disk storage capacity has not always been critical. Indeed, the first personal computers did not have disk storage. Instead, they used slow, unreliable tape cassettes. Then, in 1978, Apple demonstrated its first working prototype of the Apple

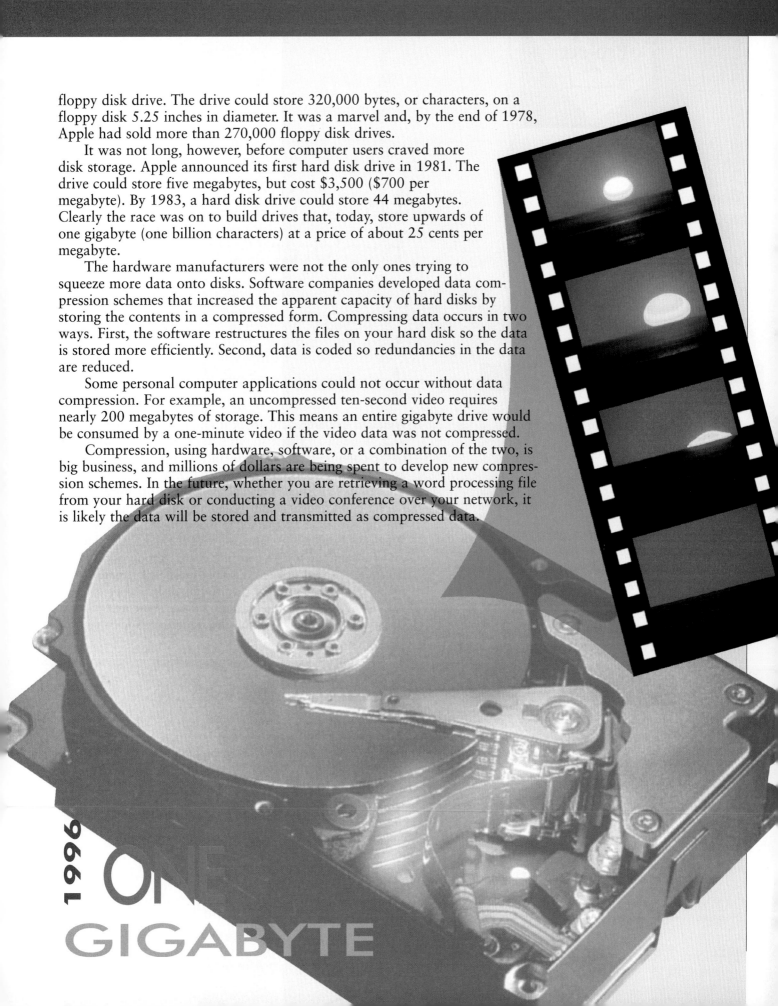

floppy disk drive. The drive could store 320,000 bytes, or characters, on a floppy disk 5.25 inches in diameter. It was a marvel and, by the end of 1978, Apple had sold more than 270,000 floppy disk drives.

It was not long, however, before computer users craved more disk storage. Apple announced its first hard disk drive in 1981. The drive could store five megabytes, but cost $3,500 ($700 per megabyte). By 1983, a hard disk drive could store 44 megabytes. Clearly the race was on to build drives that, today, store upwards of one gigabyte (one billion characters) at a price of about 25 cents per megabyte.

The hardware manufacturers were not the only ones trying to squeeze more data onto disks. Software companies developed data compression schemes that increased the apparent capacity of hard disks by storing the contents in a compressed form. Compressing data occurs in two ways. First, the software restructures the files on your hard disk so the data is stored more efficiently. Second, data is coded so redundancies in the data are reduced.

Some personal computer applications could not occur without data compression. For example, an uncompressed ten-second video requires nearly 200 megabytes of storage. This means an entire gigabyte drive would be consumed by a one-minute video if the video data was not compressed.

Compression, using hardware, software, or a combination of the two, is big business, and millions of dollars are being spent to develop new compression schemes. In the future, whether you are retrieving a word processing file from your hard disk or conducting a video conference over your network, it is likely the data will be stored and transmitted as compressed data.

1996

ONE
GIGABYTE

Microsoft
Windows 95

Using Windows Explorer

Case Perspective

Need: Your organization has finally made the decision to switch to Windows 95 from Windows 3.1. Although most everyone is excited about the change, many are apprehensive about file management. Few of them ever felt comfortable with Windows 3.1 File Manager and, as a result, hardly ever used it. Your boss has read in computer magazines that in order to effectively use Windows 95, people must learn Windows Explorer. She has asked you to teach a class with an emphasis on file management to all employees who will be using Windows 95. Your goal in Project 2 is to become competent using Windows Explorer so you can teach the class.

Introduction

Windows Explorer is an application program included with Windows 95 that allows you to view the contents of the computer, the hierarchy of folders on the computer, and the files and folders in each folder.

Windows Explorer also allows you to organize the files and folders on the computer by copying and moving the files and folders. In this project, you will use Windows Explorer to (1) work with the files and folders on your computer; (2) select and copy a group of files between the hard drive and a floppy disk; (3) create, rename, and delete a folder on floppy disk; and (4) rename and delete a file on floppy disk. These are common operations that you should understand how to perform.

Starting Windows 95

As explained in Project 1, when you turn on the computer, an introductory screen consisting of the Windows 95 logo and the Microsoft Windows 95 name displays on a blue sky and clouds background. The screen clears and Windows 95 displays several items on the desktop.

If the Welcome to Windows screen displays on your desktop, click the Close button on the title bar to close the screen. Six icons (My Computer, Network Neighborhood, Inbox, Recycle Bin, The Microsoft Network, and My Briefcase) display along the left edge of the desktop, the Microsoft Office Manager toolbar displays in the upper right corner of the desktop, and the taskbar displays along the bottom of the desktop (Figure 2-1).

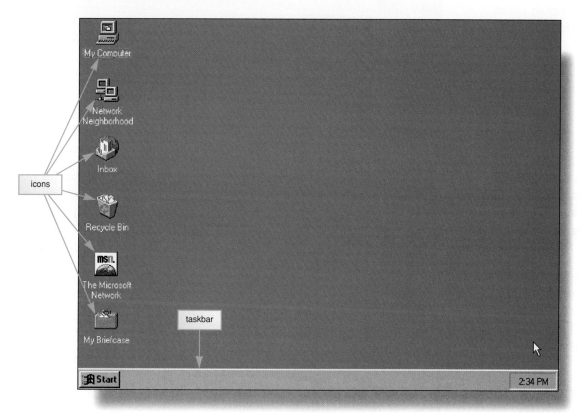

FIGURE 2-1

Starting Windows Explorer and Maximizing Its Window

To start Windows Explorer and explore the files and folders on the computer, right-click the My Computer icon on the desktop, which opens a context-sensitive menu, and then click the Explore command on the menu to open the Exploring – My Computer window. To maximize the Exploring – My Computer window, click the Maximize button on the title bar.

Steps To Start Windows Explorer and Maximize Its Window

1 Right-click the My Computer icon to open a context-sensitive menu, and then point to the Explore command on the menu.

Windows 95 highlights the My Computer icon, opens a context-sensitive menu, and highlights the Explore command on the menu (Figure 2-2). The mouse pointer points to the Explore command on the menu.

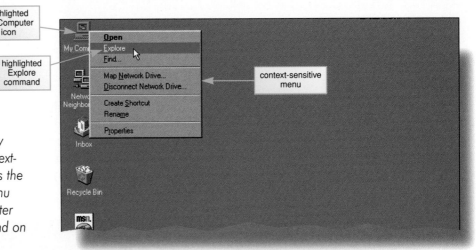

FIGURE 2-2

2 Click Explore on the context-sensitive menu, and then click the Maximize button on the Exploring – My Computer title bar.

Windows 95 opens and maximizes the Exploring – My Computer window and adds the indented Exploring – My Compu... button to the taskbar (Figure 2-3).

OtherWays

1. Right-click Start button, click Explore on context-sensitive menu
2. Click Start button, point to Programs, click Windows Explorer on the Programs submenu
3. Right-click Network Neighborhood icon, or Inbox icon, or Recycle Bin icon, or The Microsoft Network icon, or My Briefcase icon, click Explore on context-sensitive menu
4. Right-click Start button or any icons in 3 above, press E

FIGURE 2-3

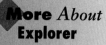

Windows Explorer

When you start Windows Explorer by right-clicking the My Computer icon, Windows 95 opens the Exploring – My Computer window (Figure 2-4). The menu bar contains the File, Edit, View, Tools, and Help menu names.

These menus contain commands to organize and work with the drives on the computer and the files and folders on those drives.

Below the menu bar is a toolbar. The **toolbar** contains a drop-down list box and thirteen buttons. The drop-down list box contains an icon and the My Computer folder name. The entry in the drop-down list box, called the **current folder**, indicates Windows Explorer was started by right-clicking the My Computer icon. The buttons on the toolbar provide a quick way to perform commonly used tasks in Windows Explorer. Many of the buttons correspond to the commands available from the menu bar. Pointing to a button on the toolbar displays a ToolTip identifying the button. If the toolbar does not display in the Exploring – My Computer window on your computer, click View on the menu bar and then click Toolbar on the View menu.

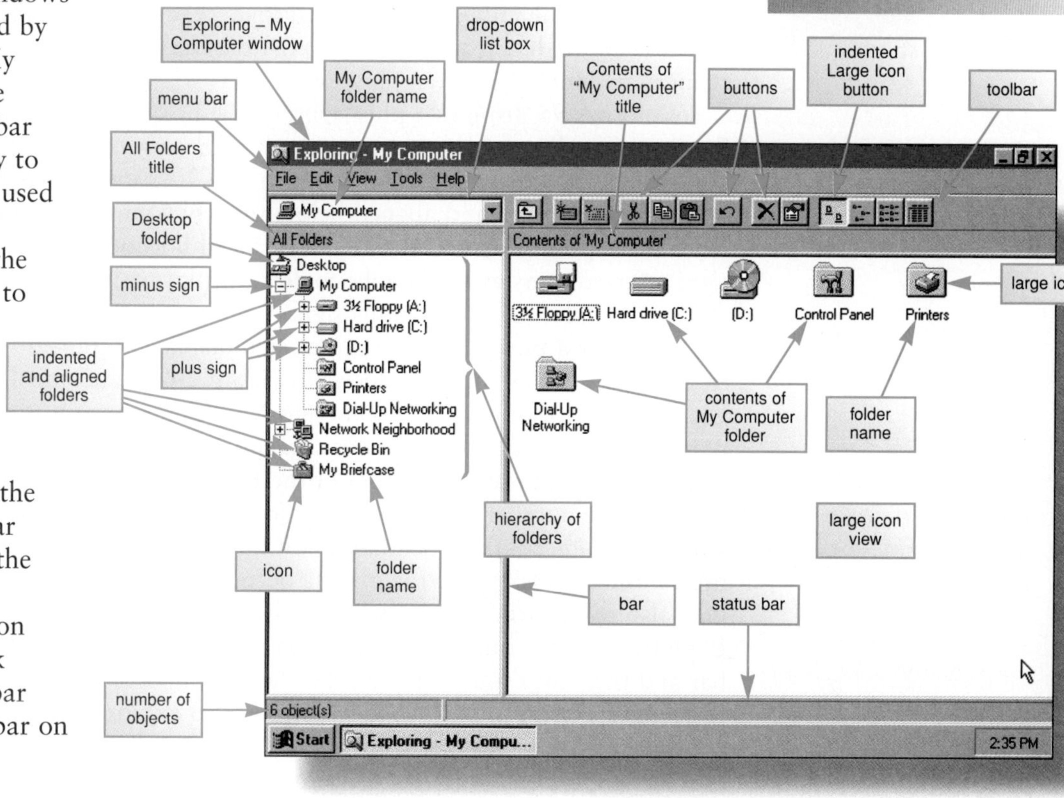

The window is divided into two areas separated by a bar. The left side of the window, identified by the All Folders title, contains a **hierarchy** of folders on the computer. The right side of the window, identified by the Contents of 'My Computer' title, displays the contents of the current folder (My Computer). In Figure 2-4, the Contents side contains the icons and folder names of six folders (3½ Floppy [A:], Hard drive [C:], and [D:], Control Panel, Printers, and Dial-Up Networking). These folders may be different on your computer. You change the size of the All Folders and Contents sides of the window by dragging the bar that separates the two sides.

Each folder in the All Folders side of the window is represented by an icon and folder name. The first folder, consisting of an icon and the Desktop folder name, represents the desktop of the computer. The four folders indented and aligned below the Desktop folder name (My Computer, Network Neighborhood,

FIGURE 2-4

More *About* Explorer

For those familiar with Windows 3.1, Windows 95 Explorer bears some resemblance to File Manager. Microsoft, however, made significant improvements and changed the basic way the program works. Those who passionately disliked File Manager might find Explorer a better way to perform file maintenance.

More *About* a Hierarchy

One definition of hierarchy in Webster's Ninth New Collegiate Dictionary is, "a division of angels." While no one would argue angels have anything to do with Windows 95, some preach that working with a hierarchical structure as presented by Explorer is less secular ("of or relating to the worldly") and more spiritual ("of or relating to supernatural phenomena") than the straight-forward showing of files in windows. What do you think?

Recycle Bin, and My Briefcase) are connected to the vertical line below the Desktop icon. These folders correspond to four of the six icons displayed on the left edge of the desktop (see Figure 2-1 on page WIN 2.5). These folders may be different on your computer.

Windows 95 displays a minus sign (–) in a box to the left of any icon in the All Folders side to indicate the corresponding folder contains one or more folders that are visible in the All Folders side. These folders, called **subfolders**, are indented and aligned below the folder name.

In Figure 2-4 on the previous page, a minus sign precedes the My Computer icon, and six subfolders are indented and display below the My Computer folder name. The six subfolders (3½ Floppy [A:], Hard drive [C:], [D:], Control Panel, Printers, and Dial-Up Networking) correspond to the six folders in the Contents side. Clicking the minus sign, referred to as **collapsing the folder**, removes the indented subfolders from the hierarchy of folders in the All Folders side and changes the minus sign to a plus sign.

Windows 95 displays a plus sign (+) in a box to the left of an icon to indicate the corresponding folder consists of one or more subfolders that are not visible in the All Folders side of the window. In Figure 2-4, a plus sign precedes the first three icons indented and aligned below the My Computer name (3½ Floppy [A:], Hard drive [C:], [D:]) and the Network Neighborhood icon. Clicking the plus sign, referred to as **expanding the folders**, displays a list of indented subfolders and changes the plus sign to a minus sign.

If neither a plus sign nor a minus sign displays to the left of an icon, the folder does not contain subfolders. In Figure 2-4, the Control Panel, Printers, Dial-Up Networking, Recycle Bin, and My Briefcase icons are not preceded by a plus or minus sign and do not contain subfolders.

The status bar at the bottom of the Exploring – My Computer window indicates the number of folders, or objects, displayed in the Contents side of the window (6 object(s)). Depending upon the objects displayed in the Contents side, the amount of disk space the objects occupy and the amount of unused disk space may also display on the status bar. If the status bar does not display in the Exploring – My Computer window on your computer, click View on the menu bar and then click Status Bar on the View menu.

In addition to using Windows Explorer to explore your computer by right-clicking the My Computer icon, you can also use Windows Explorer to explore different aspects of your computer by right-clicking the Start button on the taskbar and the Network Neighborhood, Inbox, Recycle Bin, The Microsoft Network, and My Briefcase icons on the desktop.

Displaying the Contents of a Folder

In Figure 2-4 on the previous page, the current folder (My Computer) displays in the drop-down list box on the toolbar and the Contents side of the window contains the subfolders in the My Computer folder. In addition to displaying the contents of the My Computer folder, the contents of any folder in the All Folders side can be displayed in the Contents side. Perform the following steps to display the contents of the Hard drive [C:] folder.

Steps To Display the Contents of a Folder

1 Point to the Hard drive [C:] folder name in the All Folders side of the Exploring – My Computer window (Figure 2-5).

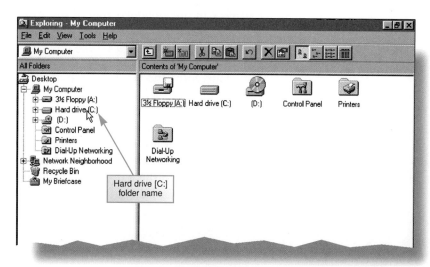

FIGURE 2-5

2 Click the Hard drive [C:] folder name.

Windows 95 highlights the Hard drive [C:] folder name in the All Folders side, changes the current folder in the drop-down list box to the Hard drive [C:] folder, displays the contents of the Hard drive [C:] folder in the Contents side, changes the window title to contain the current folder name (Exploring – Hard drive [C:]), changes the button on the taskbar to contain the current folder name, and changes the messages on the status bar (Figure 2-6). The status bar messages indicate there are 82 objects and 19 hidden objects in the Hard drive [C:] folder, the objects occupy 25.9MB of disk space, and the amount of unused disk space is 12.5MB. The contents of the Hard drive [C:] folder may be different on your computer.

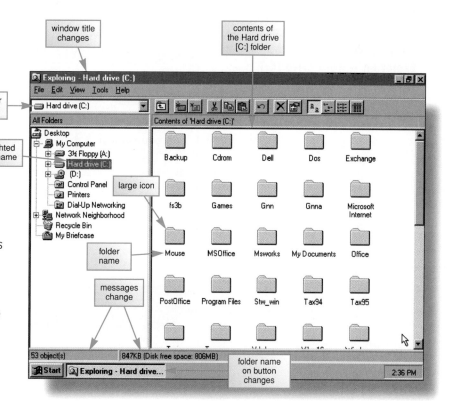

FIGURE 2-6

▶**Other**Ways

1. Double-click Hard disk [C:] icon in Contents side
2. Press TAB until any icon in All Folders side highlighted, press DOWN ARROW or UP ARROW until Hard disk [C:] highlighted in Contents side

In addition to displaying the contents of the Hard drive [C:] folder, you can display the contents of the other folders by clicking the corresponding icon or folder name in the All Folders side. The contents of the folder you click will then display in the Contents side of the window.

Expanding a Folder

Currently, the Hard drive [C:] folder is highlighted in the All Folders side of the Exploring – Hard drive [C:] window and the contents of the Hard drive [C:] folder display in the Contents side of the window. Windows 95 displays a plus sign (+) to the left of the Hard drive [C:] icon to indicate the folder contains subfolders that are not visible in the hierarchy of folders in the All Folders side of the window. To expand the Hard drive [C:] folder and display its subfolders, click the plus sign to the left of the Hard drive [C:] icon. Perform the following steps to expand the Hard drive [C:] folder.

Steps **To Expand a Folder**

1 **Point to the plus sign to the left of the Hard drive [C:] icon in the All Folders side of the Exploring – Hard drive [C:] window (Figure 2-7).**

mouse pointer points to plus sign

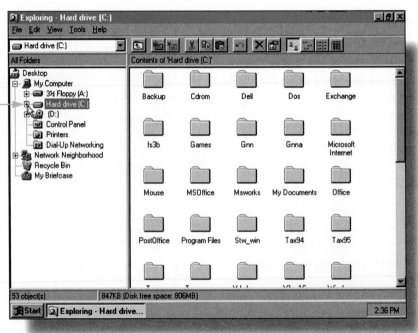

FIGURE 2-7

2 **Click the plus sign to display the subfolders in the Hard drive [C:] folder.**

Windows 95 replaces the plus sign preceding the Hard drive [C:] icon with a minus sign, displays a vertical scroll bar, and expands the Hard drive [C:] folder to include its subfolders, indented and aligned below the Hard drive [C:] folder name, (Figure 2-8). Each subfolder in the Hard drive [C:] folder is identified by a closed folder icon and folder name. The window title, current folder in the drop-down list box on the toolbar, and the files and folders in the Contents side of the window remain unchanged.

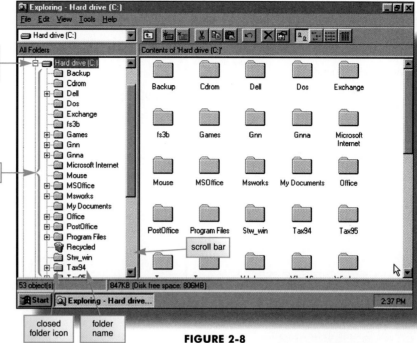

FIGURE 2-8

*Other***Ways**

1. Double-click the folder icon
2. Select folder to expand, press PLUS on numeric keypad
3. Select folder to expand, press RIGHT ARROW

Collapsing a Folder

Currently, the subfolders in the Hard drive [C:] folder display indented and aligned below the Hard drive [C:] folder name (see Figure 2-8). Windows 95 displays a minus sign (–) to the left of the Hard drive [C:] icon to indicate the folder is expanded. To collapse the Hard drive [C:] folder and then remove its subfolders from the hierarchy of folders in the All Folders side, click the minus sign preceding the Hard drive [C:] icon. Perform the following steps to collapse the Hard drive [C:] folder.

 Steps **To Collapse a Folder**

1 **Point to the minus sign preceding the Hard drive [C:] icon in the All Folders side of the Exploring – Hard drive [C:] window (Figure 2-9).**

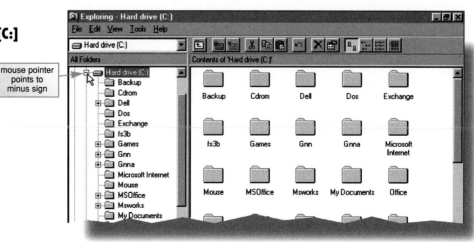

FIGURE 2-9

2 **Click the minus sign to display the Hard drive [C:] folder without its subfolders.**

Windows 95 replaces the minus sign preceding the Hard drive [C:] icon with a plus sign and removes the subfolders in the Hard drive [C:] folder from the hierarchy of folders (Figure 2-10).

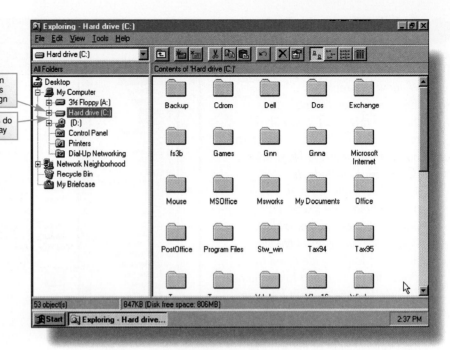

FIGURE 2-10

OtherWays

1. Highlight folder icon, press MINUS SIGN on numeric keypad
2. Double-click the folder icon
3. Select folder to collapse, press LEFT ARROW

Copying Files to a Folder on a Floppy Disk

One common operation that every student should understand how to perform is copying a file or group of files from one disk to another disk or from one folder to another folder. On the following pages, you will create a new folder, named My Files, on the floppy disk in drive A, select a group of files in the Windows folder on drive C, and copy the files from the Windows folder on drive C to the My Files folder on drive A.

When copying files, the drive and folder containing the files to be copied are called the **source drive** and **source folder**, respectively. The drive and folder to which the files are copied are called the **destination drive** and **destination folder**, respectively. Thus, the Windows folder is the source folder, drive C is the source drive, the My Files folder is the destination folder, and drive A is the destination drive.

Creating a New Folder

In preparation for selecting and copying files from a folder on the hard drive to a folder on the floppy disk in drive A, a new folder with the name of My Files will be created on the floppy disk. Perform the following steps to create the new folder.

Steps **To Create a New Folder**

1 Insert a formatted floppy disk into drive A on your computer.

2 Click the 3½ Floppy [A:] folder name in the All Folders side of the Exploring – Hard drive [C:] window and then point to an open area of the Contents side of the window.

Windows 95 highlights the 3½ Floppy [A:] folder name, changes the current folder to 3½ Floppy [A:], displays the contents of the 3½ Floppy [A:] folder in the Contents side, and changes the messages on the status bar (Figure 2-11). The window title, Contents side title, and button on the taskbar change to include the 3½ Floppy [A:] folder name. Currently, no files or folders display in the Contents side. The files and folders may be different on your computer. The mouse pointer points to an open area of the Contents side.

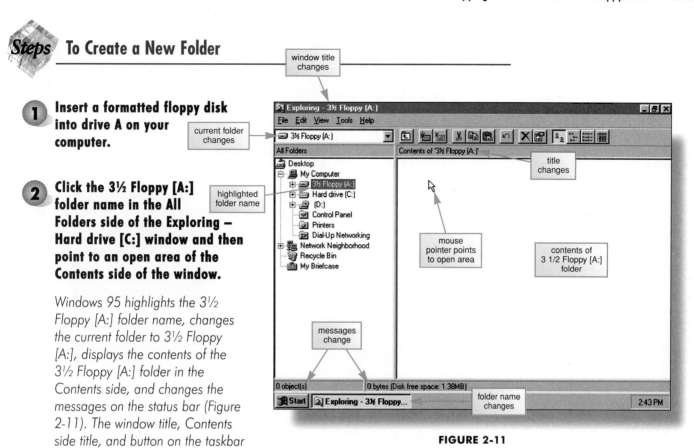

FIGURE 2-11

3 Right-click the open area of the Contents side of the window to open a context-sensitive menu and then point to New on the menu.

Windows 95 opens a context-sensitive menu and the New sub-menu, highlights the New command in the context-sensitive menu, and displays a message on the status bar (Figure 2-12). The message, Contains commands for creating new items., indicates the New submenu contains commands that allow you to create new items in the Contents side. The mouse pointer points to the New command. Although no subfolders display in the Contents side and no plus sign should precede the 3½ Floppy [A:] icon in the All Folders area, a plus sign precedes the icon.

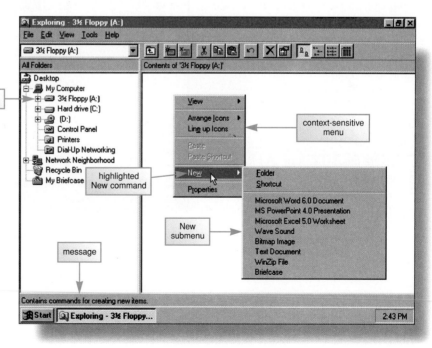

FIGURE 2-12

Point to Folder on the New submenu.

Windows 95 highlights the Folder command on the New submenu and displays the message, Creates a new, empty folder., on the status bar (Figure 2-13). The mouse pointer points to the Folder command. Clicking the Folder command will create a folder in the Contents side of the window using the default folder name, New Folder.

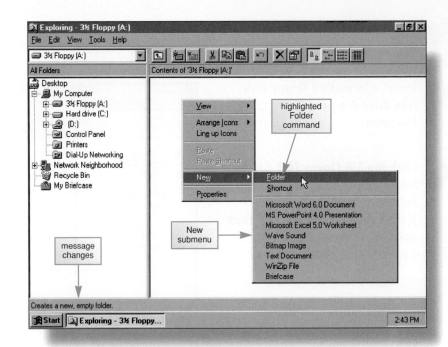

FIGURE 2-13

Click Folder on the New submenu.

Windows 95 closes the context-sensitive menu and New submenu, displays the highlighted New Folder icon in the Contents side, and changes the message on the status bar (Figure 2-14). The text box below the icon contains the highlighted default folder name, New Folder, followed by the insertion point. A plus sign continues to display to the left of the 3½ Floppy [A:] icon to indicate the 3½ Floppy [A:] folder contains the New Folder subfolder. The message on the status bar indicates one object is selected in the Contents side.

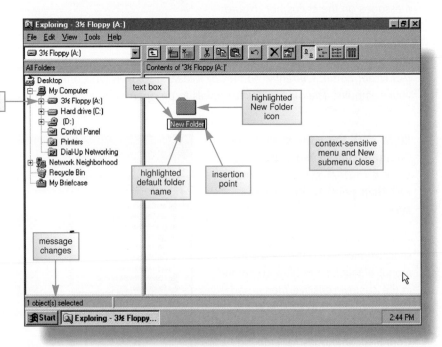

FIGURE 2-14

6 **Type** My Files **in the text box and then press the ENTER key.**

The new folder name, My Files, is entered and Windows 95 removes the text box (Figure 2-15).

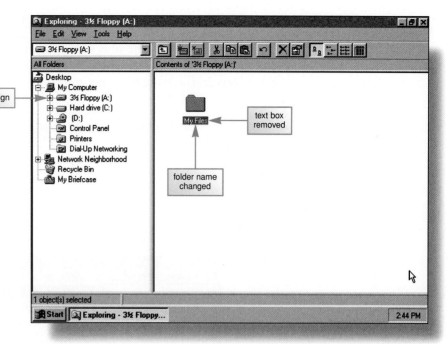

plus sign

text box removed

folder name changed

FIGURE 2-15

Other Ways

1. Select drive, click File on the menu bar, on File menu click New, click Folder on New submenu

After creating the My Files folder on the floppy disk in drive A, you can save files in the folder or copy files from other folders to the folder. On the following pages, you will copy a group of files consisting of the Black Thatch, Bubbles, and Circles files from the Windows folder on drive C to the My Files folder on drive A.

Displaying the Destination Folder

To copy the three files from the Windows folder on drive C to the My Files folder on drive A, the files to be copied will be selected in the Contents side and right-dragged to the My Files folder in the All Folders side. Prior to selecting or right-dragging the files, the destination folder (My Files folder on drive A) must be visible in the All Folders side and the three files to be copied must be visible in the Contents side.

Currently, the plus sign (+) to the left of the 3½ Floppy [A:] icon indicates the folder contains one or more subfolders that are not visible in the All Folders side (see Figure 2-15). Perform the steps on the next page to expand the 3½ Floppy [A:] folder to display the My Files subfolder.

TO EXPAND THE 3½ FLOPPY [A:] FOLDER

Step 1: Point to the plus sign to the left of the 3½ Floppy [A:] icon in the All Folders side of the Exploring – 3½ Floppy [A:] window.

Step 2: Click the plus sign to display the subfolders in the 3½ Floppy [A:] folder.

Windows 95 replaces the plus sign preceding the 3½ Floppy [A:] folder with a minus sign, highlights the 3½ Floppy [A:] folder name, and displays the subfolders in the 3½ Floppy [A:] folder, indented and aligned below the 3½ Floppy [A:] folder name (Figure 2-16). Currently, only one subfolder (My Files) displays.

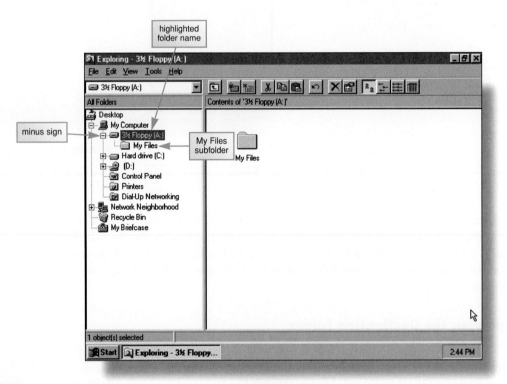

FIGURE 2-16

Other Ways

1. Right-click 3½ Floppy [A:] icon, click Explore

Displaying the Contents of the Windows Folder

Currently, the My Files folder displays in the Contents side of the Exploring – 3½ Floppy [A:] window. To copy files from the source folder (Windows folder on drive C) to the My Files folder, the Windows folder must be visible in the All Folders side. To make the Windows folder visible, you must expand the Hard drive [C:] folder, scroll the All Folders side to make the Windows folder name visible, and then click the Windows folder name to display the contents of the Windows folder in the Contents side. Perform the following steps to display the contents of the Windows folder.

Steps **To Display the Contents of a Folder**

1 **Click the plus sign to the left of the Hard drive [C:] icon in the All Folders side of the Exploring – 3½ Floppy [A:] window, scroll the All Folders side to make the Windows folder name visible, and then point to the Windows folder name.**

*Windows 95 replaces the plus sign to the left of the Hard drive [C:] icon with a minus sign, displays the subfolders in the Hard drive [C:] folder, and scrolls the hierarchy of folders in the All Folders side to make the Windows folder visible (Figure 2-17). In addition to folders and other files, the Windows folder contains a series of predefined graphics, called **clip art files**, that can be used with application programs. The mouse pointer points to the Windows folder name. The plus sign to the left of the Hard drive [C:] icon is not visible in Figure 2-17.*

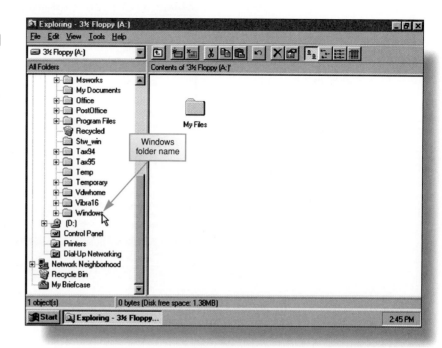

FIGURE 2-17

2 **Click the Windows folder name to display the sub-folders in the Windows folder.**

Windows 95 highlights the Windows folder name in the All Folders side of the window, changes the closed folder icon to the left of the Windows folder name to an open folder icon, and displays the contents of the Windows folder in the Contents side (Figure 2-18).

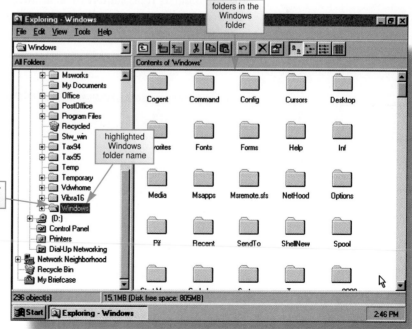

FIGURE 2-18

3 Scroll the Contents side to make the files in the Windows folder visible.

One folder (Wordview folder) and several files display in the Contents side of the window (Figure 2-19). Each file is identified by a large icon and a filename. The files and folders in the Windows folder may be different and the file extensions may not display on your computer.

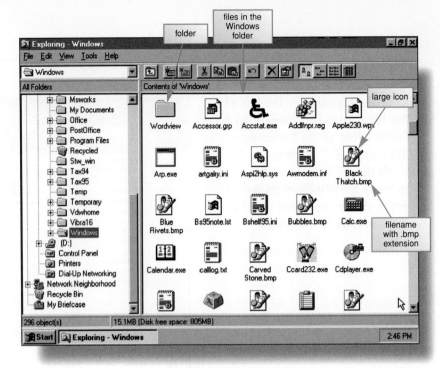

FIGURE 2-19

Changing the View

In Figure 2-19, the files and folder in the Contents side of the Exploring – Windows window display in large icons view. In **large icons view**, each file and folder is represented by a large icon and a filename or folder name. Other views include the small icons, list, and details views. The list view is often useful when copying or moving files from one location to another location. In **list view**, each file or folder is represented by a smaller icon and name, and the files and folders are arranged in columns. Perform the following steps to change from large icons view to list view.

Steps **To Change to List View**

1 **Right-click any open area in the Contents side of the Exploring – Windows window to open a context-sensitive menu, point to View on the context-sensitive menu, and then point to List on the View submenu.**

Windows 95 opens a context-sensitive menu, highlights the View command on the context-sensitive menu, opens the View submenu, and highlights the List command on the View submenu (Figure 2-20). A large dot to the left of the Large Icons command on the View submenu indicates files and folders in the Contents side display in large icons view. The mouse pointer points to the List command. Clicking the List command will display the files and folders in the Contents side in list view.

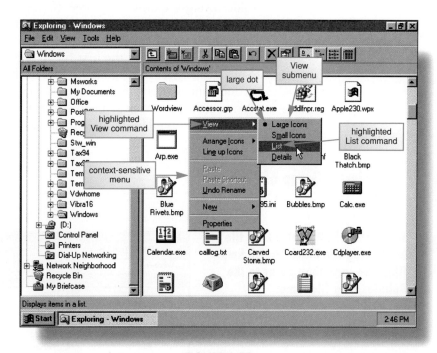

FIGURE 2-20

2 **Click List on the View submenu.**

Windows 95 displays the files and folders in the Contents side of the window in list view, indents the List button on the toolbar, and returns the Large Icons button to normal (Figure 2-21).

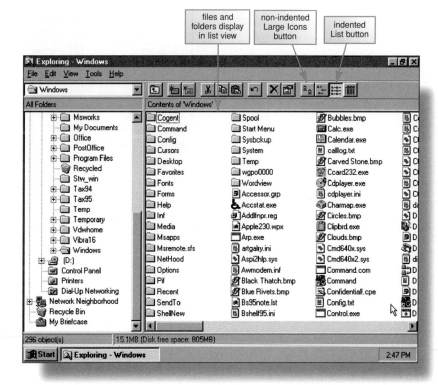

FIGURE 2-21

OtherWays
1. On View menu click List
2. Click List button on toolbar
3. Press ALT+V, press L

Selecting a Group of Files

You can easily copy a single file or group of files from one folder to another folder using Windows Explorer. To copy a single file, select the file in the Contents side of the window and right-drag the highlighted file to the folder in the All Folders side where the file is to be copied. Group files are copied in a similar fashion. Select the first file in a group of files by clicking its icon or filename. You select the remaining files in the group by pointing to each file icon or filename, holding down the CTRL key, and clicking the file icon or filename. Perform the following steps to select the group of files consisting of the Black Thatch.bmp, Bubbles.bmp, and Circles.bmp files.

Steps **To Select a Group of Files**

1 **Select the Black Thatch.bmp file by clicking the Black Thatch.bmp filename, and then point to the Bubbles.bmp filename.**

Windows highlights the Black Thatch.bmp file in the Contents side and displays two messages on the status bar (Figure 2-22). The messages indicate that one file is selected (1 object(s) selected) and the size of the file (182 bytes). The mouse pointer points to the Bubbles.bmp filename.

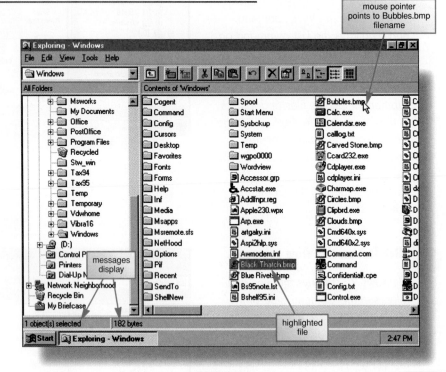

FIGURE 2-22

2 Hold down the CTRL key, click the Bubbles.bmp filename, release the CTRL key, and then point to the Circles.bmp filename.

The Black Thatch.bmp and Bubbles.bmp files are highlighted, and the two messages on the status bar change to reflect the additional file selected (Figure 2-23). The messages indicate that two files are selected (2 object(s) selected) and the size of the two files (2.24KB). The mouse pointer points to the Circles.bmp filename.

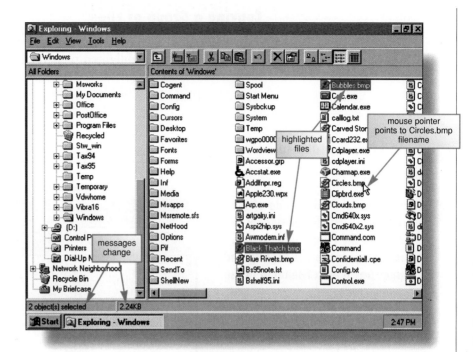

FIGURE 2-23

3 Hold down the CTRL key, click the Circles.bmp filename, and then release the CTRL key.

The group of files consisting of the Black Thatch.bmp, Bubbles.bmp, and Circles.bmp files is highlighted, and the messages on the status bar change to reflect the selection of a third file (Figure 2-24). The messages indicate that three files are selected (3 object(s) selected) and the size of the three files (2.43KB).

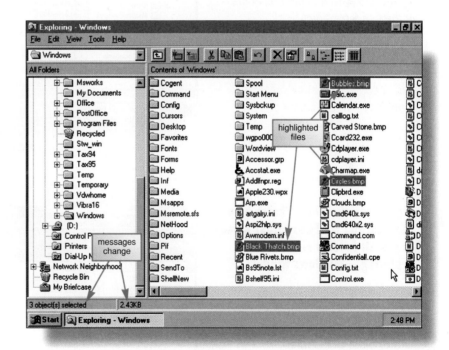

FIGURE 2-24

*Other*Ways

1. Use arrow keys to select first file, hold down SHIFT key to move to next file, press SPACEBAR

2. To select contiguous files, select first filename, hold down SHIFT key, click last filename

3. To select all files, click Edit on menu bar, click Select All

Copying a Group of Files

After selecting a group of files, copy the files to the My Files folder on drive A by pointing to any highlighted filename in the Contents side, and right-dragging the filename to the My Files folder in the All Folders side. Perform the following steps to copy a group of files.

 To Copy a Group of Files

1 **Scroll the All Folders side of the Exploring – Windows window to make the My Files folder visible and then point to the highlighted Black Thatch.bmp filename in the Contents side.**

Windows 95 scrolls the All Folders side to make the My Files folder visible (Figure 2-25). The mouse pointer points to the highlighted Black Thatch.bmp filename in the Contents side.

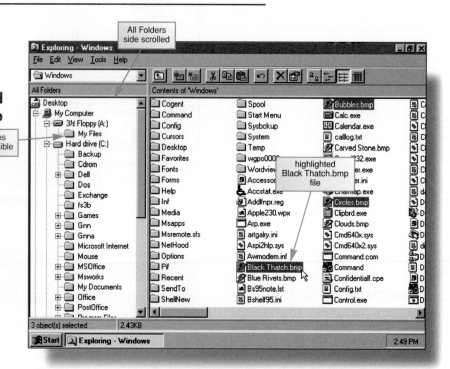

FIGURE 2-25

2 **Right-drag the Black Thatch.bmp file over the My Files folder name in the All Folders side of the Exploring – Windows window.**

As you drag the file, Windows 95 displays an outline of an icon and a horizontal line of one or more of the three files being copied and highlights the My Files folder name (Figure 2-26). The mouse pointer contains a plus sign to indicate the group of files is being copied, not moved.

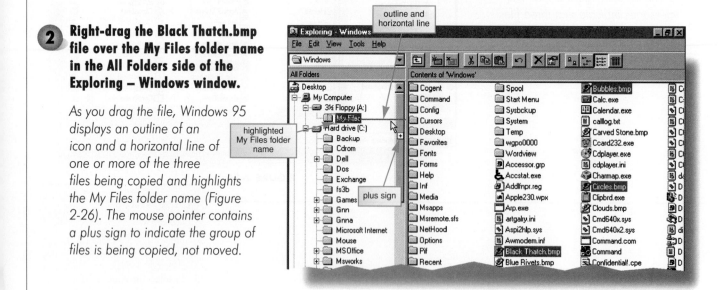

3 Release the right mouse button to open a context-sensitive menu, and then point to the Copy Here command on the menu.

Windows 95 opens a context-sensitive menu and highlights the Copy Here command on the menu (Figure 2-27). The mouse pointer points to the Copy Here command. Clicking the Copy Here command will copy the three files to the My Files folder.

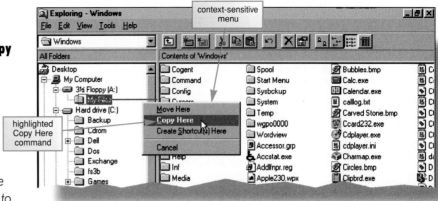

FIGURE 2-27

4 Click Copy Here on the context-sensitive menu.

Windows 95 opens the Copying dialog box, and the dialog box remains on the screen while Windows 95 copies each file to the My Files folder (Figure 2-28). The Copying dialog box shown in Figure 2-28 indicates the Black Thatch.bmp file is currently being copied.

FIGURE 2-28

> **Other Ways**
> 1. Right-drag file to copy from Contents side to folder icon in All Folders side, click Copy on context-sensitive menu
> 2. Select file to copy in Contents side, click Edit on menu bar, click Copy on Edit menu, select folder icon to receive copy, click Edit on menu bar, click Paste on Edit menu

Displaying the Contents of the My Files Folder

After copying a group of files, you should verify that the files were copied into the correct folder. To view the files that were copied to the My Files folder, click the My Files folder name in the All Folders side.

More About Copying and Moving

"Copying, moving, it's all the same to me," you might be tempted to say. They're not the same at all! When you copy a file, it will be located at two different places - the place it was copied to and the place it was copied from. When a file is moved, it will be located at only one place - where it was moved to. Many users have been sorry they did not distinguish the difference when a file they thought they had copied was moved instead.

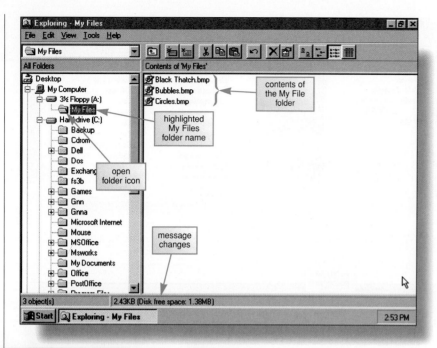

FIGURE 2-29

TO DISPLAY THE CONTENTS OF A FOLDER

Step 1: Point to the My Files folder name in the All Folders side of the Exploring – Windows window.

Step 2: Click the My Files folder name in the All Folders side.

Windows 95 highlights the My Files folder name in the All Folders side, replaces the closed folder icon to the left of the My Files folder name with an open folder icon, displays the contents of the My Files folder in the Contents side, and changes the message on the status bar (Figure 2-29). The status bar message indicates 1.38MB of free disk space on the disk in drive A.

More *About*
Renaming a File or Folder

A file or folder name can contain up to 255 characters, including spaces. But, they cannot contain any of the following characters: \ /:*?"<>|.

Renaming a File or Folder

Sometimes, you may want to rename a file or folder on disk. You change the filename by clicking the filename twice, typing the new filename, and pressing the ENTER key. Perform the following steps to change the name of the Circles.bmp file on drive A to Blue Circles.bmp.

Steps **To Rename a File**

1 **Point to the Circles.bmp filename in the Contents side.**

The mouse pointer points to the Circles.bmp filename (Figure 2-30).

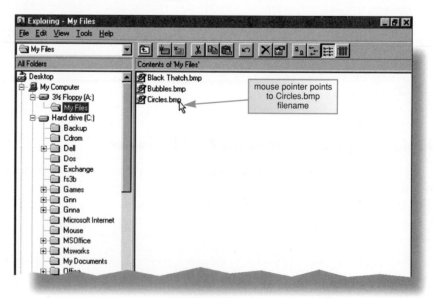

FIGURE 2-30

2 Click the Circles.bmp filename twice (do not double-click the filename).

Windows 95 displays a text box containing the highlighted Circles.bmp filename and insertion point (Figure 2-31).

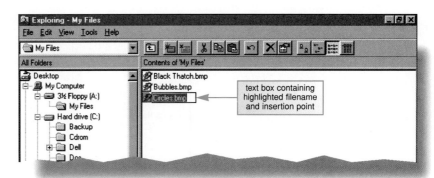

FIGURE 2-31

3 Type Blue Circles.bmp and then press the ENTER key.

Windows 95 changes the filename to Blue Circles.bmp and removes the box surrounding the filename (Figure 2-32).

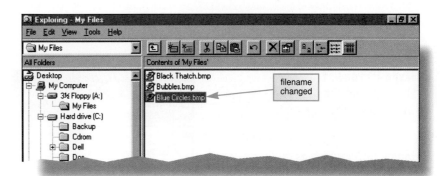

FIGURE 2-32

OtherWays

1. Right-click filename in Contents side, click Rename on context-sensitive menu, type name, press ENTER
2. Select filename in Contents side, click File on menu bar, click Rename on File menu, type name, press ENTER

To change a folder name, click the folder name twice, type the new folder name, and press the ENTER key. Perform the steps below and on the next page to change the name of the My Files folder to Clip Art Files.

 Steps To Rename a Folder

1 Point to the My Files folder name in the All Folders side of the Exploring – My Files window.

The mouse pointer points to the My Files folder name (Figure 2-33).

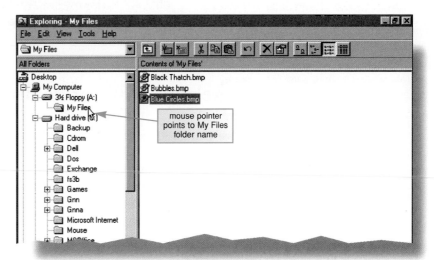

FIGURE 2-33

2 Click the My Files folder name twice (do not double-click the folder name).

Windows 95 displays a text box containing the highlighted My Files name and insertion point (Figure 2-34).

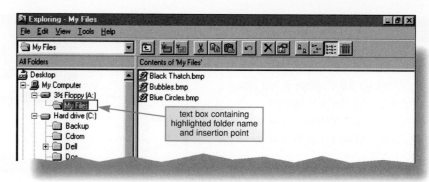

FIGURE 2-34

3 Type Clip Art Files **and then press the ENTER key.**

Windows 95 changes the folder name to Clip Art Files and removes the box surrounding the folder name (Figure 2-35). The new folder name replaces the old folder name in the window title, drop-down list box, Contents side title, and button on the taskbar.

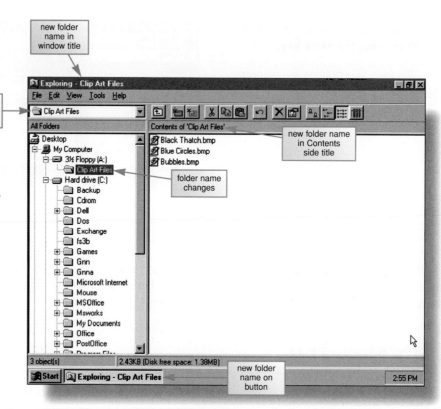

FIGURE 2-35

OtherWays

1. Click folder name, press F2, type new name, press ENTER
2. Click folder name, click File on menu bar, click Rename, type new name, press ENTER

Deleting a File or Folder

When you no longer need a file or folder, you can delete it. Two methods are commonly used to delete a file or folder. One method uses the Delete command on the context-sensitive menu that opens when you right-click the filename or folder name. Another method involves right-dragging the unneeded file or folder to the **Recycle Bin**. The Recycle Bin icon is located at the left edge of the desktop (see Figure 2-1 on page WIN 2.5).

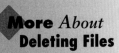

When you delete a file or folder on the hard drive using the Recycle Bin, Windows 95 stores the deleted file or folder temporarily in the Recycle Bin until you permanently discard the contents of the Recycle Bin by emptying the Recycle Bin. Until the Recycle Bin is emptied, you can retrieve the files and folders you deleted in error. Unlike deleting files or folders on the hard drive, when you delete a file or folder located on a floppy disk, the file or folder is deleted immediately and not stored in the Recycle Bin.

On the following pages, you will delete the Bubbles.bmp and Black Thatch.bmp files. The Bubbles.bmp file will be deleted by right-clicking the Bubbles.bmp filename and then clicking the Delete command on a context-sensitive menu. Next, the Black Thatch.bmp file will be deleted by dragging the Black Thatch.bmp file to the Recycle Bin.

Deleting a File by Right-Clicking Its Filename

To delete a file using the Delete command on a context-sensitive menu, right-click the filename in the Contents side to open a context-sensitive menu and then click the Delete command on the menu. To illustrate how to delete a file by right-clicking, perform the steps below and on the next page to delete the Bubbles.bmp file.

 Steps To Delete a File by Right-Clicking

1 **Right-click the Bubbles.bmp filename in the Contents side of the Exploring – Clip Art Files window and then point to the Delete command on the context-sensitive menu.**

Windows 95 opens a context-sensitive menu and highlights the Bubbles.bmp filename (Figure 2-36). The mouse pointer points to the Delete command on the menu.

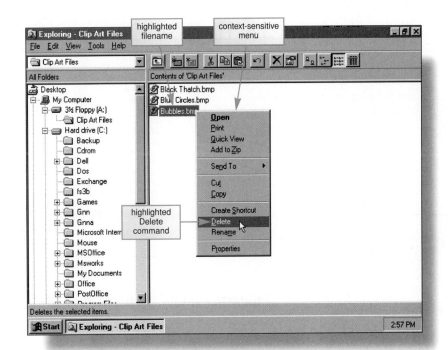

FIGURE 2-36

More *About*
Deleting Files

A few years ago, someone proposed that the Delete command be removed from operating systems. It seems an entire database was deleted by an employee who thought he knew what he was doing, resulting in a company that could not function for more than a week while the database was rebuilt. Millions of dollars in revenue were lost. The Delete command is still around, but it should be considered a dangerous weapon.

2 Click Delete on the context-sensitive menu. When the Confirm File Delete dialog box opens, point to the Yes button.

Windows 95 opens the Deleting dialog box and then opens a Confirm File Delete dialog box on top of the Deleting dialog box (Figure 2-37). The Confirm File Delete dialog box contains the message, Are you sure you want to delete 'Bubbles.bmp'?, and the Yes and No command buttons. The mouse pointer points to the Yes button. Clicking the Yes button confirms the deletion of the Bubbles.bmp file and causes the file to be deleted.

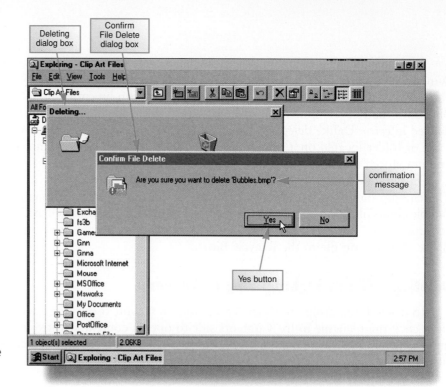

FIGURE 2-37

3 Click the Yes button in the Confirm File Delete dialog box.

Windows 95 closes the Confirm File Delete dialog box, displays the Deleting dialog box while the file is being deleted, and then removes the Bubbles.bmp file from the Contents side (Figure 2-38).

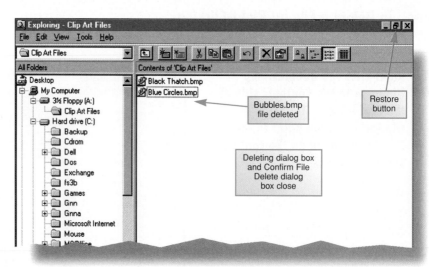

FIGURE 2-38

OtherWays
1. Click filename, press DELETE

More *About* Deleting Files

Warning! This is your last warning! Be EXTREMELY careful when deleting files. Hours and weeks of hard work can be lost with one click of a button. If you are going to delete files or folders from your hard disk, consider making a backup of those files so that if you inadvertently delete something you need, you will be able to recover.

Deleting a File by Right-Dragging Its Filename

Another method to delete a file is to right-drag the filename from the Contents side of the window to the Recycle Bin icon on the desktop to open a context-sensitive menu, and then click the Move Here command on the context-sensitive menu. Currently, the Exploring – Clip Art Files window is maximized and occupies the entire desktop. With a maximized window, you cannot right-drag a file to the Recycle Bin. To allow you to right-drag a file, restore the Exploring – Clip Art Files window to its original size by clicking the Restore button on the title bar. Perform the following steps to delete the Black Thatch.bmp file by right-dragging its filename.

Steps To Delete a File by Right-Dragging

1 **Click the Restore button on the Exploring – Clip Art Files window title bar and then point to the Black Thatch.bmp filename in the Contents side of the window.**

Windows 95 restores the Exploring – Clip Art Files window to its original size before maximizing the window and replaces the Restore button on the title bar with the Maximize button (Figure 2-39). The mouse pointer points to the Black Thatch.bmp filename in the Contents side of the window.

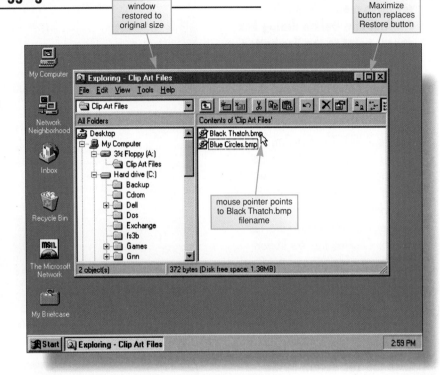

FIGURE 2-39

2 **Right-drag the Black Thatch.bmp filename over the Recycle Bin icon, and then point to the Move Here command on the context-sensitive menu.**

Windows 95 opens a context-sensitive menu and highlights the Move Here command on the menu (Figure 2-40). The Black Thatch.bmp filename displays on top of the Recycle Bin icon on the desktop and the mouse pointer points to the Move Here command on the menu.

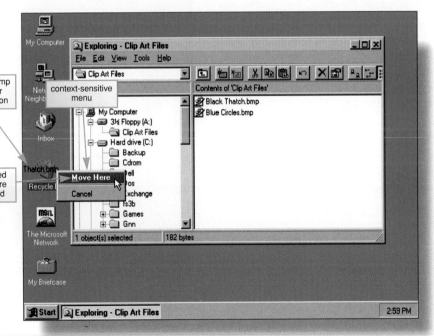

FIGURE 2-40

3 **Click Move Here on the context-sensitive menu. When the Confirm File Delete dialog box opens, point to the Yes button.**

Windows 95 opens the Deleting dialog box and then opens the Confirm File Delete dialog box on top of the Deleting dialog box (Figure 2-41). The Confirm File Delete dialog box contains the message, Are you sure you want to delete 'Black Thatch.bmp'?, and the Yes and No command buttons. The mouse pointer points to the Yes button. Clicking the Yes button confirms the deletion of the Black Thatch.bmp file and causes the file to be deleted.

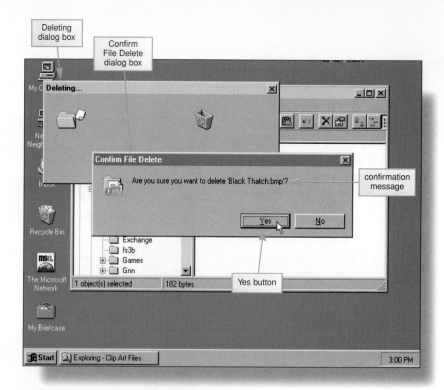

FIGURE 2-41

4 **Click the Yes button in the Confirm File Delete dialog box.**

Windows 95 closes the Confirm File Delete dialog box, displays the Deleting dialog box while the file is being deleted, and then removes the Black Thatch.bmp file from the Contents side (Figure 2-42).

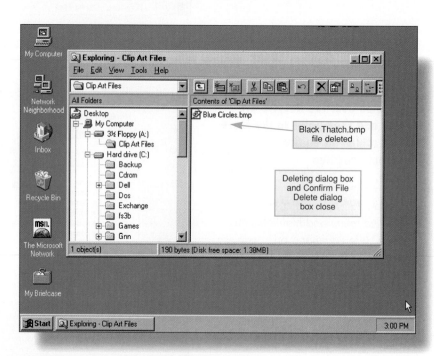

FIGURE 2-42

More *About* **the Recycle Bin**

Once you delete a file or folder, it's gone forever – True or False? Windows stores deleted files and folders in the Recycle Bin. You can recover files or folders you delete in error using the Recycle Bin.

Whether you delete a file by right-clicking or right-dragging, you can use the file selection techniques illustrated earlier in this project to delete a group of files. When deleting a group of files, click the Yes button in the Confirm Multiple File Delete dialog box to confirm the deletion of the group of files.

Deleting a Folder

When you delete a folder, Windows 95 deletes any files or subfolders in the folder. You can delete a folder using the two methods shown earlier to delete files (right-clicking or right-dragging). Perform the steps below and on the next page to delete the Clip Art Files folder on drive A by right-dragging the folder to the Recycle Bin.

▶ **More** *About*
Deleting Folders

If you drag a folder to the Recycle Bin, only the files in that folder appear in the Recycle Bin. If you restore a file that was originally located in a deleted folder, Windows recreates the folder, and then restores the file to it.

Steps **To Delete a Folder**

1 Point to the Clip Art Files folder name in the All Folders side of the Exploring – Clip Art Files window (Figure 2-43).

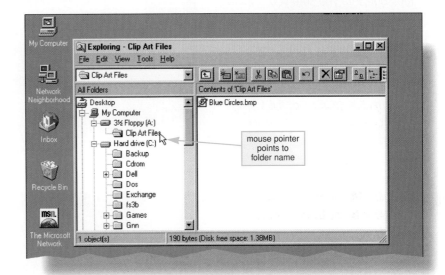

FIGURE 2-43

2 Right-drag the Clip Art Files icon in the All Folders side to the Recycle Bin icon, and then point to the Move Here command on the context-sensitive menu.

Windows 95 opens a context-sensitive menu (Figure 2-44). The mouse pointer points to the highlighted Move Here command on the menu.

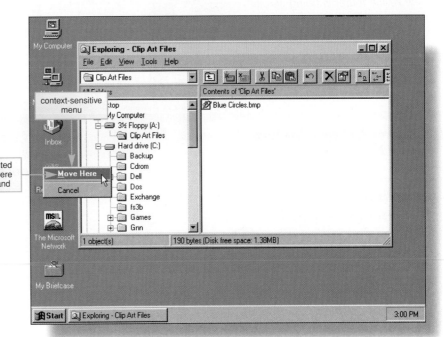

FIGURE 2-44

3 **Click Move Here on the context-sensitive menu. When the Confirm Folder Delete dialog box opens, point to the Yes button.**

Windows 95 opens the Deleting dialog box and then opens the Confirm Folder Delete dialog box on top of the Deleting dialog box (Figure 2-45). The Confirm Folder Delete dialog box contains the message, Are you sure you want to remove the folder 'Clip Art Files' and all its contents?, and the Yes and No command buttons. The mouse pointer points to the Yes button. Clicking the Yes button confirms the deletion of the Clip Art Files folder and causes the folder and its contents to be deleted.

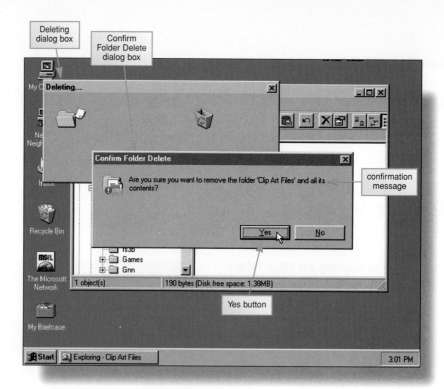

FIGURE 2-45

4 **Click the Yes button in the Confirm Folder Delete dialog box.**

Windows 95 closes the Confirm Folder Delete dialog box, displays the Deleting dialog box while the folder is being deleted, removes the Clip Art Files folder from the All Folders side, and replaces the minus sign preceding the 3½ Floppy [A:] icon with a plus sign (Figure 2-46).

5 **Remove the floppy disk from drive A.**

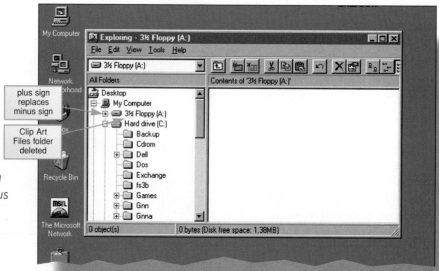

FIGURE 2-46

Other Ways
1. Click folder name, press DELETE

Quitting Windows Explorer and Shutting Down Windows 95

After completing work with Windows Explorer, quit Windows Explorer using the Close button on the Windows Explorer title bar, and then shut down Windows using the Shut Down command on the Start menu.

Perform the following steps to quit Windows Explorer.

TO QUIT AN APPLICATION

Step 1: Point to the Close button in the Exploring window.
Step 2: Click the Close button.

Windows 95 closes the Windows Explorer window and quits Windows Explorer.

Perform the following steps to shut down Windows 95.

TO SHUT DOWN WINDOWS 95

Step 1: Click the Start button on the taskbar.
Step 2: Click Shut Down on the Start menu.
Step 3: Click the Yes button in the Shut Down Windows dialog box.
Step 4: Turn off the computer.

Project Summary

In this project, you used Windows Explorer to select and copy a group of files, change views, display the contents of a folder, create a folder, expand and collapse a folder and rename and delete a file and a folder.

What You Should Know

Having completed this project, you should now be able to perform the following tasks:

- Change to List View *(WIN 2.19)*
- Collapse a Folder *(WIN 2.11)*
- Copy a Group of Files *(WIN 2.22)*
- Create a New Folder *(WIN 2.13)*
- Delete a File by Right-Clicking *(WIN 2.27)*
- Delete a File by Right-Dragging *(WIN 2.29)*
- Delete a Folder *(WIN 2.31)*
- Display the Contents of a Folder *(WIN 2.9, WIN 2.17, WIN 2.24)*
- Expand a Folder *(WIN 2.10)*
- Expand the 3½ Floppy [A:] Folder *(WIN 2.16)*
- Quit an Application *(WIN 2.33)*
- Rename a File *(WIN 2.24)*
- Rename a Folder *(WIN 2.25)*
- Select a Group of Files *(WIN 2.20)*
- Shut Down Windows 95 *(WIN 2.33)*
- Start Windows Explorer and Maximize Its Window *(WIN 2.6)*

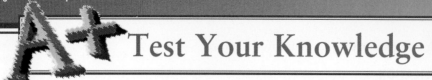

Test Your Knowledge

1 True/False

Instructions: Circle T if the statement is true or F if the statement is false.

T F 1. Windows Explorer is an application you can use to organize and work with the files and folders on the computer.

T F 2. Double-clicking the My Computer icon is the best way to open Windows Explorer.

T F 3. The contents of the current folder are displayed in the All Folders side.

T F 4. To display the contents of drive C on your computer in the Contents side, click the plus sign in the small box next to the drive C icon.

T F 5. A folder that is contained within another folder is called a subfolder.

T F 6. To display the contents of a folder, right-click its folder name.

T F 7. Collapsing a folder removes the subfolders from the hierarchy of folders in the All Folders side.

T F 8. After you expand a drive or folder, the information in the Contents side is always the same as the information displayed below the drive or folder icon in the All Folders side.

T F 9. The source folder is the folder containing the files to be copied.

T F 10. You select a group of files in the Contents side by pointing to each icon or filename and clicking the left mouse button.

2 Multiple Choice

Instructions: Circle the correct response.

1. The drop-down list box in the Exploring - My Computer window contains the
   _____.
   a. hierarchy of folders
   b. source folder
   c. files in the current folder
   d. current folder

2. The _____ contains the hierarchy of folders on the computer.
   a. Contents side
   b. status bar
   c. All Folders side
   d. toolbar

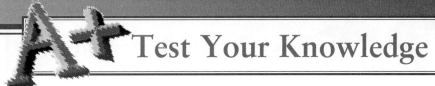

3. To display the contents of a folder in the Contents side, _____.
   a. double-click the plus sign next to the folder icon
   b. right-click the folder icon in the All Folders side
   c. click the folder icon in the Contents side
   d. click the folder icon in the All Folders side

4. You _____ the minus sign preceding a folder icon to expand a folder.
   a. click
   b. drag
   c. double-click
   d. point to

5. When an expanded file is collapsed in the All Folders side, _____.
   a. the expansion closes and the contents of the folder display in the Contents side
   b. the entire Exploring - My Computer window closes
   c. the computer beeps at you because you cannot perform this activity
   d. the My Computer window opens

6. To select multiple files in the Contents side, _____.
   a. right-click each file icon
   b. hold down the SHIFT key and then click each file icon you want to select
   c. hold down the CTRL key and then click each file icon you want to select
   d. hold down the CTRL key and then double-click each file icon you want to select

7. After selecting a group of files, you _____ the group to copy the files to a new folder.
   a. click
   b. right-drag
   c. double-click
   d. none of the above

8. In _____ view, each file or folder in the Contents side is represented by a smaller icon, and the files or folders are arranged in columns.
   a. large icons
   b. small icons
   c. list
   d. details

9. A file or folder can be renamed by _____.
   a. right-dragging its filename
   b. double-clicking its filename
   c. dragging its filename
   d. clicking its filename twice

(continued)

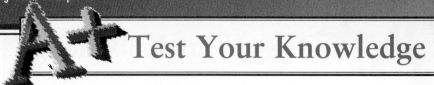

Test Your Knowledge

Multiple Choice *(continued)*

10. A file can be deleted by right-dragging the filename from the Contents side of the window to the
    _____ icon on the desktop.
    a. My Computer
    b. Network Neighborhood
    c. Recycle Bin
    d. My Briefcase

3 Understanding the Exploring - My Computer Window

Instructions: In Figure 2-47 arrows point to several items in the Exploring - My Computer window. Identify the items or objects in the spaces provided.

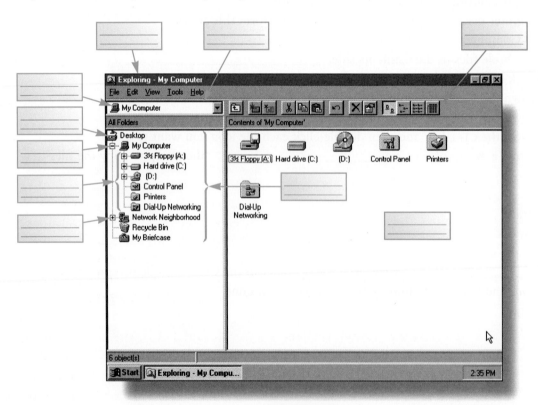

FIGURE 2-47

1 Using Windows Help

Instructions: Use Windows Help and a computer to perform the following tasks.

1. Start Microsoft Windows 95 if necessary.
2. Answer the following questions about paths.
   a. What is a path? _____
   b. What does a path include? _____
   c. How do you specify a path? _____
   d. What do you do if your filename contains more than eight characters? _____
3. Open the Help Topics: Windows Help window. Click the Index tab if necessary and then type `windows explorer` in the text box. Click demo in the Windows Explorer list and then click the Display button. In the Windows Help window, play the demonstration.
   a. How does the demonstration open Windows Explorer? _____
   b. What folders are contained on drive C in the demonstration? _____
4. How can you cause Explorer to start each time you start Windows 95? _____
5. You have recently written a business letter to a manager named Lori Hill. You explained CD-ROM drives to her. You want to see what else you said in the letter, but you can neither remember the name of the file nor where you stored the file on your computer. You read something in your Windows 95 manual that the Find command could be used to find lost files. Using Help, determine what you must do to find your letter. Write those steps in the spaces provided.

   _____

   _____

   _____

6. You and a friend both recently bought computers. She was lucky and received a color printer as her birthday gift. You would like to print some of your more colorful documents on her color printer. You have heard that for not too much money you can buy a network card and some cable and hook up your computers on a network. Then, you can print documents stored on your computer on her color printer. Using Windows Help, determine if you can share her printer. If so, what must you do in Windows 95 to make this become a reality. Print the Help pages that document your answer.
7. You can hardly believe that last week you won a laptop computer at a charity dance. The application programs on the laptop are the same as those on your desktop computer. The only trouble is that when you use your laptop computer to modify a file, you would like the same file on your desktop also to be modified. In that way, you can work on the file either on your desktop computer or on your laptop computer. A friend mentioned that the My Briefcase feature of Windows 95 allows you to do what you want to do. Using Windows Help, find out all you can about My Briefcase. Print the Help pages that specify how to keep files on both your desktop and laptop computers synchronized with each other.

In the Lab

1 File and Program Properties

Instructions: Use a computer to perform the following tasks and answer the questions.

1. Start Microsoft Windows 95 if necessary.
2. Open the My Computer window.
3. Open the drive C window on your computer.
4. Scroll until the Windows icon is visible in the drive C window.
5. Right-click the Windows icon.
6. Click Open on the context-sensitive menu.
7. Scroll until the Black Thatch icon is visible. If the Black Thatch icon does not display on your computer, find another Paint icon.
8. Right-click the Black Thatch icon.
9. Click Properties on the context-sensitive menu.
10. Answer the following questions about the Black Thatch file:
    a. What type of file is Black Thatch? _____
    b. What is the path for the location of the Black Thatch file? (Hint: Point to the location of the file)

       _____
    c. What is the size (in bytes) of the Black Thatch file? _____
    d. What is the MS-DOS name of the Black Thatch file? _____ The tilde (~) character
       is placed in the MS-DOS filename when the Windows 95 filename is greater than 8 characters.
       Windows 95 uses the first six characters of the long filename, the tilde character, and a number
       to distinguish the file from other files that might have the same first six characters.
    e. When was the file created? _____
    f. When was the file last modified? _____
    g. When was the file last accessed ? _____
11. Click the Cancel button in the Black Thatch Properties dialog box.
12. Scroll in the Windows window until the Notepad icon displays.
13. Right-click the Notepad icon.
14. Click Properties on the context-sensitive menu.
15. Answer the following questions:
    a. What type of file is Notepad? _____
    b. What is the path of the Notepad file? _____
    c. How big is the Notepad file? _____
    d. What is the file extension of the Notepad file? What does it stand for?

       _____
    e. What is the file version of the Notepad file? _____
    f. What is the file's description? _____
    g. Who is the copyright owner of Notepad? _____
    h. What language is Notepad written for? _____
16. Click the Cancel button in the Notepad Properties dialog box.
17. Close all open windows.

In the Lab

2 Windows Explorer

Instructions: Use a computer to perform the following tasks:

1. Start Microsoft Windows 95.
2. Right-click the My Computer icon.
3. Click Explore on the context-sensitive menu.
4. Maximize the Exploring window.
5. Drag the bar between the All Folders side and the Contents side to the center of the Exploring window. What difference do you see in the Window? _____
   _____
6. Return the bar to its previous location.
7. Click Tools on the menu bar.
8. Click Go to on the Tools menu.
9. Type c:\windows and then click the OK button in the Go To Folder dialog box. What happened in the Exploring window? _____
10. Click View on the menu bar and then click Small Icons on the View menu.
11. Click View on the menu bar and then click Options on the View menu.
12. Drag the Options dialog box so you can see the Contents side of the Exploring window. Click Show all files. Click the Apply button. Do any more folders display? If so, what new folders display? Did more files display?
    _____
    _____
13. Click Hide files of these types. Click Hide MS-DOS file extensions for file types that are registered. Click the Apply button. Did the filenames displayed in the Contents area change? If so, what are the changes? Give three examples of filenames that are different:
    _____
    _____
14. Click Hide MS-DOS file extensions for file types that are registered. Click Hide files of these types. Click the OK button.
15. Click View on the menu bar and then click Details on the View menu.
    a. In the Contents side, scroll until you see only file icons and then click the Name button below the Contents of 'Windows' bar. Did the sequence of file icons change? How?
       _____
    b. Click the Size button. How did the sequence of file icons change? _____
    c. Click the Type button. How did the sequence of file icons change? _____
    d. Click the Modified button. How did the sequence of folder and file icons change?
       _____
    e. Click the Name button.

(continued)

In the Lab

Windows Explorer *(continued)*

16. Click Edit on the menu bar. Click Select All on the Edit menu. If the Select All dialog box displays, click the OK button. What happened? _____

17. Click Edit on the menu bar. Click Invert Selection on the Edit menu. Was there any change? _____

18. Click File on the menu bar. Point to New on the File menu and then click Bitmap Image on the New submenu. What happened? _____

19. Type In the Lab Image and then press the ENTER key. What is the name of the bitmap image? _____

20. Right-click the In the Lab Image icon. Click Delete on the context-sensitive menu. Click the Yes button in the Confirm File Delete dialog box.

21. Close the Exploring window.

3 Window Toolbars

Instructions: Use a computer to perform the following tasks:

1. Open the My Computer window.
2. Maximize the My Computer window.
3. Click View on the menu bar. Click Large icons on the View menu.
4. Click View on the menu bar. If a check does not display to the left of the Toolbar command, click Toolbar on the View menu. A toolbar displays in the My Computer window (Figure 2-48).
5. Click the down arrow next to the drop-down list box containing the My Computer icon and name.
6. Click the drive C icon in the drop-down list. How did the window change? _____ _____
7. Double-click the Windows icon. What happened? _____ _____
8. In the Windows window, if the toolbar does not display, click View on the menu bar and then click Toolbar on the View menu.
9. Scroll down if necessary until the Argyle icon displays in the window. If the Argyle icon does not display on your computer, find another Paint icon. Click the Argyle icon and then point to the Copy button on the toolbar (Hint: To determine the function of each button on the toolbar, point to the button).
10. Click the Copy button. Do you see any change? If so, what? _____

In the Lab

11. Insert a formatted floppy disk in drive A of your computer.

12. Click the down arrow next to the drop-down list box containing the Windows icon and name.

13. Click the 3½ Floppy [A:] icon in the drop-down list. What happened? _____

14. If the toolbar does not display in the 3½ Floppy [A:] window, click View on the menu bar and then click Toolbar on the View menu.

15. In the 3½ Floppy [A:] window, click the Paste button on the toolbar. The Argyle icon displays in the 3½ Floppy [A:] window.

16. With the Argyle icon highlighted in the 3½ Floppy [A:] window, click the Delete button on the toolbar and then click the Yes button in the Confirm File Delete dialog box.

17. In the 3½ Floppy [A:] window, return the toolbar status to what it was prior to step 8. Close the 3½ Floppy [A:] window.

18. In the drive C window, click the Small Icons button and then describe the screen. _____
_____

19 Click the List button and then describe the screen. _____

20. Click the Details button and then describe the screen. _____

21. Click the Large Icons button on the toolbar

22. Click the Up One Level button on the toolbar. What is the difference between clicking the Up One Level button and clicking My Computer in the drop-down list box? _____

23. Return the toolbar status to what it was prior to step 4. Close the My Computer and drive C windows.

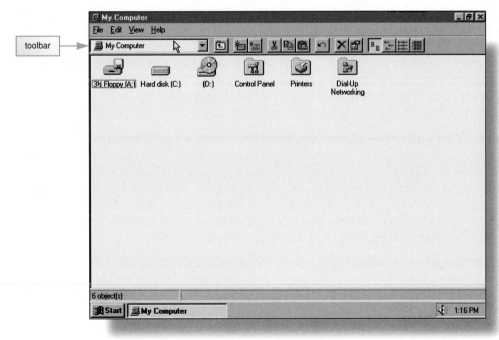

FIGURE 2-48

Cases and Places

200 MHz

The difficulty of these case studies varies:

◗ Case studies preceded by a single half moon are the least difficult. You can complete these case studies using your own computer in the lab.

◗◗ Case studies preceded by two half moons are more difficult. You must research the topic presented using the Internet, a library, or another resource, and then prepare a brief written report.

◗◗◗ Case studies preceded by three half moons are the most difficult. You must visit a store or business to obtain the necessary information, and then use it to create a brief written report.

1 ◗ A key feature of Windows 95 is the capability to modify the view of a window to suit individual preferences and needs. Using Windows Explorer, display the Hard drive [C:] folder in the Contents side and then experiment with the different commands on the View menu. Describe the effects of the Large Icons, Small Icons, List, and Details commands on the icons in the Contents side. When using details view, explain how clicking one of the buttons at the top of the Contents side (such as Name or Type) changes the window. Try out diverse arrangements of icons on the Contents side by pointing to the Arrange Icons command on the View menu and then clicking various commands on the Arrange Icons submenu. Finally, specify situations in which you think some of the views you have seen would be most appropriate.

2 ◗ When the Hard disk [C:] folder is displayed in the Contents side of the Exploring window, it is clear that an enormous number of folders and files are stored on your computer's hard disk. Imagine how hard it would be to manually search through all the folders and files to locate a specific file! Fortunately, Windows 95 provides the Find command to perform the search for you. Click Tools on the Exploring window menu bar, point to Find, and then click Files or Folders on the Find submenu. Learn about each sheet in the Find: All Files dialog box by clicking a tab (Name & Location, Date Modified, or Advanced), clicking the Help menu, clicking What's This? on the Help menu, and then clicking an item on a sheet. Try finding a file using each sheet. Finally, explain how the Find command is used and describe a circumstance in which each sheet would be useful. When you are finished, click the Close button on the window title bar to close the Find: All Files dialog box.

3 ◗◗ Backing up files is an important way to protect data and ensure it is not inadvertently lost or destroyed. File backup on a personal computer can use a variety of devices and techniques. Using the Internet, a library, personal computer magazines, or other resources, determine the types of devices used to store backed up data, the schedules, methods, and techniques for backing up data, and the consequences of not backing up data. Write a brief report of your findings.

Cases and Places

4 ▶▶ A hard disk must be maintained in order to be used most efficiently. This maintenance includes deleting old files, defragmenting a disk so it is not wasteful of space, and from time to time finding and attempting to correct disk failures. Using the Internet, a library, Windows 95 Help, or other research facilities, determine the maintenance that should be performed on hard disks, including the type of maintenance, when it should be performed, how long it takes to perform the maintenance, and the risks, if any, of not performing the maintenance. Write a brief report on the information you obtain.

5 ▶▶▶ The quest for more and faster disk storage continues as application programs grow larger and create sound and graphic files. One technique for increasing the amount of data that can be stored on a disk is disk compression. Disk compression programs, using a variety of mathematical algorithms, store data in less space on a hard disk. Many companies sell software you can load on your computer to perform the task. Windows 95 has disk compression capabilities as part of the operating system. Visit a computer store and find two disk compression programs you can buy. Write a brief report comparing the two packages to the disk compression capabilities of Windows 95. Discuss the similarities and differences between the programs and identify the program that claims to be the most efficient in compressing data.

6 ▶▶▶ Some individuals in the computer industry think both the Windows 3.1 and the Windows 95 operating systems are deficient when it comes to ease of file management. Therefore, they have developed and marketed software that augments the operating systems to provide different and, they claim, improved services for file management. Visit a computer store and inquire about products such as Symantec's Norton Navigator for Windows 95. Write a brief report comparing the products you tested with Windows 95. Explain which you prefer and why.

7 ▶▶▶ Data stored on disk is one of a company's more valuable assets. If that data were to be stolen, lost, or compromised so it could not be accessed, the company could literally go out of business. Therefore, companies go to great lengths to protect their data. Visit a company or business in your area. Find out how it protects its data against viruses, unauthorized access, and even against such natural disasters as fire and tornadoes. Prepare a brief report that describes the procedures. In your report, point out any areas where you see the company has not adequately protected its data.

Index